Johann Baptist Wirthmüller

Die moralische Tugend der Religion

in ihren unmittelbaren Akten und Gegensätzen

Johann Baptist Wirthmüller

Die moralische Tugend der Religion
in ihren unmittelbaren Akten und Gegensätzen

ISBN/EAN: 9783743645264

Hergestellt in Europa, USA, Kanada, Australien, Japan

Cover: Foto ©Lupo / pixelio.de

Weitere Bücher finden Sie auf **www.hansebooks.com**

The Situation in China

A Report to the Board of Foreign Missions of
the Methodist Episcopal Church of
an Official Visit by

REV. RALPH E. DIFFENDORFER, D.D.

Corresponding Secretary

PRESENTED TO THE EXECUTIVE COMMITTEE OF THE BOARD
JULY 21, 1927
NEW YORK CITY

THE SITUATION IN CHINA

It was not until we reached Manila, on March 31, and met there our missionaries from South China that we had any intimation whatever of the extent, significance, and effect of recent events in China. Throughout our three and one-half months of journeying in India, except for occasional reflections in the periodicals from America, always four to six weeks old, we would not have known that there was anything unusual happening in China. Short paragraphs in the press from Reuter's brought the only news we had; "General So-and-So advanced—"; "The Powers were in Conference—," etc. The nationalist press in India, dependent upon the same source, with bits of information secured through their own channels, confined themselves largely to comments on the bearings of the revolution in China on their own nationalist aspirations.

When we left Burma, on February 4, we still expected to carry out our full itinerary in China. Indeed, in Burma we received letters from Bishop Wallace Brown and missionaries in Fukien outlining our itinerary for a two weeks' visit to the interior stations.

On February 7, we were in Singapore at the closing session of the Malaya Conference, and on the eleventh we left Singapore for Java. During these few days in Singapore, the report had come that Dr. Hu's hospital of the Woman's Foreign Missionary Society in Foochow had been looted and that she was probably then in Singapore. The reasons given for the attack seem to indicate no anti-foreign or anti-Christian feeling. When we returned to Singapore from Java and South Sumatra, on February 28, we had no additional information, except that letters, coming through from Chinese in South China to Chinese in Singapore, indicated that there were serious troubles in their country.

On March 5, when we visited Douglas Coole at Sitiawan in the Malay peninsula, we learned through a letter from Dr. T. H. Coole, of Foochow, who was one of the missionary refugees in Manila, that there had been a general evacuation of missionaries from South China. We then went to North Sumatra and did not again return to Singapore until March 17, and left for North Borneo and the Philippines on March 19, a twelve days' voyage. On March 28, at Sandakan, North Borneo, after we had embarked on an Australian boat for Manila, the wireless operator gave us a confused and garbled message concerning "the capture of Shanghai and the bombardment of the city with the loss of many Chinese and foreign lives." We discovered later that this message referred to the Nanking disaster of March 24.

The chief interest in these facts is in the way news of the upheaval in China apparently is being censored, only a slight indication of the estimate given in some quarters of the possible effect of what is happening in China on the destinies of the people of Asia and their governments.

In Manila, letters came through from Shanghai telling of the Nanking outrage and the newspapers were discussing the reaction of the Powers to the Nanking affair. During our two weeks in the Philippine Islands, our China missionaries revealed a confused and chaotic state of mind, and a wide difference of opinion as to the wisdom and necessity for the evacuation and to the possibility of return. We were getting quite opposite messages from Foochow as to the possibility of visiting Fukien at all, and finally concluded to go to Hongkong, to discover what could be done and to receive there messages as to procedure. Upon our arrival in Hongkong, a message from Bishop Brown reported that he had left Foochow for Shanghai to see Mrs. Brown on board ship for America, and suggested that we come to Shanghai for conference with a few of his men. We also had urgent appeals from our missionaries and Chinese in Foochow to make every effort to visit them. This was the Saturday before Easter. We engaged passage on a ship sailing for Foochow on the Tuesday morning after Easter, April 19. We had concluded that as long as any of our missionaries were in China and felt that they needed and desired our presence, it was the duty and the privilege of a Secretary of the Board of Foreign Missions to go to them at any cost. In the meantime the American Consul at Foochow had given his consent to our going, and later told me we had done our duty in visiting Foochow to see, for ourselves, the conditions under the new nationalist regime.

In Canton

On Saturday, in Hongkong, we found the night and day boats to Canton running, and after inquiry at the local steamship office, together with consultation with a British army officer in our hotel, the Chinese manager of our hotel, and the manager of the American Express Company, all of whom said we probably would find Canton quiet, we decided to take the Saturday night boat up the Pearl river to Canton and to spend Easter day there.

On Sunday morning, at breakfast on the boat approaching Canton, we met a refugee missionary who was just returning to Canton after several weeks' absence, to conduct the Easter services at the Church of England in Shameen, the foreign concession. This service was a Parade Service, attended by a company of British soldiers, six women and a dozen foreign civilian men. Then we went into the Chinese city to our Canton Methodist Church, for their 12 o'clock Easter service. It will be remembered that this church in Canton is an outgrowth of work among the Chinese in New York City and in California, and is independent of our Annual Conferences in China. It is now a self-supporting church and has, through its own efforts, opened eighteen preaching places and Sunday schools, some of them the beginnings of other independent congregations. We found a congregation of about seventy-five, of whom two thirds or more were men. At the close of the service, the pastor greeted me very heartily and called a young Chinese, an American-trained doctor who knew English. We were also greeted by the pastor of our Chinese congregation in Sacramento,

THE SITUATION IN CHINA 5

California, who had come to Canton to get his wife and family to take them to America. The young doctor had spent thirteen years in the United States, studying at Asbury College, Emory University, and George Washington University, having completed his medical course, with two years of interneship and a year of special training in surgery. He is now the president of the Kwong Wah Medical College in Canton, a Chinese institution independent of foreign control from the beginning, financed and built by Chinese money, entirely staffed by Chinese medical men, mostly Christians, with a student body of 150 young men and women. He is also superintendent of the medical school hospital. He and his wife invited us to lunch with them at a Chinese restaurant.

We walked up Taiping Road, a modern thoroughfare marked out and cut through the heart of the city west from the river front, one of the improvements of the commission form of government established six years ago under Dr. Sun Yat Sen. A few minutes later found us on the third floor of a large Chinese public eating house, in a little alcove behind closed screens. There, during the process of our first Chinese meal in China, this young doctor gave us our first connected account of what was happening in China. He also told us of the proclamation posted throughout the city, that on April 12 there was to begin a general massacre of all the foreigners in China, to be completed about the sixteenth, Good Friday. On the way to the restaurant we passed under bamboo arches that were being erected on main thoroughfares for the celebration of the event. Following these proclamations, there had been almost a complete exodus of foreigners from Canton. Nothing happened on the twelfth nor on any day following, until early on the morning of Good Friday, April 16, when General Chiang Kai Shek turned the tables and inaugurated his campaign to exterminate the Communist radicals from Kuomintang. It was reported that on Good Friday morning, between 200 and 300 Communists were executed in Canton, more than 1,000 were put in prison, and 1,500 labor agitators were being held prisoners in two large unfinished office buildings. On the way to our Chinese restaurant, as we turned into Taiping Road, we saw in the block ahead of us hundreds of Chinese working men filling the street. On both sides of this street, in the heart of Canton's best business district, two six-story modern office buildings were in the process of construction by a group of wealthy Chinese, each building costing about $500,000 Mex. When these buildings were nearing completion, they were taken over by the Communist laborers employed on them, and turned into living quarters and labor union headquarters. These fine new buildings gave every appearance of crowded tenements. On Friday morning, nationalist troops seized the two buildings, put guards at all the entrances, and the occupants became prisoners. On Sunday morning, as we passed through, we saw the imprisoned working men letting ropes down from the windows of the stories above, with baskets attached, and pulling up food and clothing furnished by friends on the street.

It was this campaign against the radical element that relieved the tension of the city, made it quiet and orderly, if not friendly. Seated in this Canton restaurant on Easter day, this young educated and intensely patriotic physician and surgeon gave his view of the general situation in China. In Exhibit "A," on page 37 of this report, will be found some paragraphs from the stenographic notes of this conversation.

On Sunday evening we spent several hours in conference with some of the missionaries from the Union Theological Seminary of Canton. On Monday morning we went down the river to the campus of Canton Christian College. It was guarded at all entrances by nationalist troops. We had to secure passes from the officer at the main entrance, and give up the passes upon our exit. All the members of the faculty and the president, Dr. Henry, were required to observe this rule. The university had been closed for about two weeks, due to labor difficulties. The labor group had made demand after demand which the university had met, and finally all the employees of various kinds at the university were organized into one labor union. These included the men in the pump house, the electricians, the gardeners, the servants in the homes of the faculty, both Chinese and foreign, and the clerks, stenographers and bookkeepers in the university offices.

A good illustration of labor difficulties in Canton at the present time is indicated by the situation at the college pump house. After the erection of the new pumping station, there had been employed a good, faithful Chinese to run the pumps. Some months ago he came to the university authorities and said that he would have to have another man on the pumps, that he was working too long hours, and that the labor union had decided that there should be two men for a shift instead of one. The university complied and things went along as usual. Then the two pump men came and said they would have to have a man to cook their meals for them while they were at work during the day. Again the university authorities complied. The cook was provided and the pumps were again operating, when one day it was discovered that the two pump men had retired from business and out of their salaries had employed the cook to run the pumps!

The university was finally forced to close its doors. When the announcement was made, there were over 700 students in attendance. All but a few of them voted to keep the university going, the students volunteering to do the work of the servants on the grounds. Dr. Henry pointed out that this loyalty on the part of the students shows that they have passed through a two-year period of agitation, unrest and impossible demands upon the part of the student body. The students, of course, did not find themselves capable of doing all the kinds of work that had to be done. When we visited Canton, the university was in consultation with city and labor union officials, looking toward a possible settlement. During our visit there we studied the plan for the reorganization of the university in order to meet the requirements for registration under the nationalist government, our first introduction to that problem. At the College, all the requirements had been met. There was a Chinese board of managers, a Chinese president, and a plan worked out whereby the former Board of Trustees in New York should become an American Foundation, and should, under certain conditions, rent the property in Canton to the Board of Managers in China at $1.00 a year. Dr. Henry, with far-sighted vision, has taken a lesser post in the university in order to preserve the contacts and the support of the university's American constituency. In making these adaptations, and in anticipating the revolution and its meaning for education in China, the university has not had the unanimous support of the foreign community in South China, especially in Canton and Hongkong, as we discovered in conversations with army officers and business men. Canton Christian College, now known as Lingnan University, has incurred for itself the reputation of being exceedingly "radical and unsafe," when as a matter of fact, from the point of view of the college authorities, it was merely adapting itself to inevitable conditions, and stabilizing itself in Chinese life in preparation for even larger service to the Chinese community.

Later, on Monday, we visited the Kwong Wah medical college and hospital, drove throughout the city over the newly constructed streets, saw the National University, the public parks, the playgrounds, and the fine new outdoor amphitheater and stadium, heard and discussed further plans for the development of modern sewerage and sanitation systems, health education, and other schemes of this progressive southern city.

It was interesting to us to observe that the one American woman missionary who did not leave her post in Canton is instructor in English literature at the National University. She has gone to and fro day after day to her work, and testifies that her contacts there with the nationalists are worth more to her and her future service to the Christian movement than all of her previous years in China.

We shall never cease to be grateful that our first contact with China was in Canton. It is decidedly a Chinese city, the foreign concession, Shameen, being a limited area on an island in the river. Signs of progress were in evidence everywhere. The people seemed to believe in the revolution and in the future of China. In Canton one felt the spirit of the Nationalist Movement, which was not repressed by any outside influences. The missionaries from America, England, Australia and New Zealand with whom we talked all shared this buoyant hope. While recognizing the difficulties and the excuses, they were also clear in the conviction that nothing can withstand or check the evolution of national consciousness in a great but hitherto politically dormant people.

In Foochow

The three-day sail from Hongkong to Foochow included a day's stop at Swatow and a day at Amoy. We found Swatow under martial law, the raid on the Communists having started the night before, when thirty-five were reported executed, twelve of them publicly. At Amoy, there had been executions a plenty. We went ashore but found few foreigners. On Friday morning, April 22, we were anchored in the Min River below the city of Foochow.

The missionaries from Foochow, in a special launch, gave us a welcome even before our ship from Hongkong had found suitable anchorage in the river. As we stepped to the rail, we saw a pert little steam launch making circles around us, with a dozen handkerchiefs wig-wagging an enthusiastic "Glad to see you!" What we lacked in numbers, we made up in vigor as we returned the signals.

They came up the gangway like a boarding party, and we found ourselves surrounded by a happy crowd of men and women who had been worried for fear we would be frightened out of a visit to Foochow. Visitors to Foochow were not numerous during those days of active anti-Christian and anti-foreign propaganda, and the American Consul had ordered all American women and children to leave, allowing only those men and single women to remain who were essential to the conduct of institutions.

The launch was able to take us all and our luggage, and we started from Pagoda anchorage up the twelve miles of shallow water to the city of Foochow. There were several prominent Chinese in our party, most distinguished among whom was Mr. Hu, a Christian layman of the highest quality, a gray haired man who has never had the advantage of a foreign education, but whose precise English puts to shame the slang of some of the younger generation who have returned from years of study in America.

The trip up to Foochow that day in the launch was a combination picnic and pilgrimage. We stopped first at an island where the American Board has located a splendid hospital, and met two of our own missionary families from the interior, living there under refugee conditions. In one case, a single room made dining room, living room and bed-room facilities for a family of four. Whatever the inconveniences, or whatever the uncertainties concerning the future we found no bitterness of resentment against the Chinese people. Our second stop was about noon, on another island which was occupied by a small fishing village, and where we had some good Chinese food for which Foochow is famous. Our third stop was half-way to Foochow at the campus of Fukien Christian University, the beautiful new buildings with Chinese architecture which we had seen on their high promontory long before we reached the landing place. After a brief stop we started off again toward our destination, the large island of Nan Tai in the Min River, opposite the old walled city of Foochow.

Just as our launch got out into mid-stream, some one spied a familiar Chinese figure hurrying along the bank, and we turned back to pick up Ding Nguong Lung, teacher at the university and pastor of our fine congregation at the Church of the Heavenly Rest, in the city of Foochow. It was our first meeting with the man whose life has been threatened, against whom proclamations have been posted, and who recently had to flee into the country and remain in hiding after an anti-foreign mob had broken into his home, searching for him, stealing some of his private possessions and badly frightening his wife and children. Less than thirty-five years of age, this young preacher, with the best training of Syracuse and Columbia universities to his credit, has gone into his pulpit Sunday after Sunday in the face of hysterical

THE SITUATION IN CHINA

opposition in the non-Christian community and preached a social gospel that demanded the application of the principles of Jesus to the present difficulties in China. He is a marked man, marked as a target for those who are out to "get" anyone who holds an opinion different from their own, and marked for a place of prophetic leadership in the future Church of China.

Our chief topic of conversation on the launch was whether or not the Christian institutions ought to register under the educational requirements of the new government, and we found that in the Foochow community this was the subject of greatest moment not only to the missionary leaders of our Methodist institutions, but to the Chinese pastors, the Chinese staffs of those institutions, and above all to the students. This question has become one of those concrete issues which determine in times of transition whether one is "for" or "against" a regime.

The conditions under which a school is permitted to register, briefly, are (1) a Chinese president; (2) a Chinese board of managers; (3) voluntary religious instruction; and (4) party education for the Kuomintang to be carried on within the school.* There would be little or no question about the acceptance of these condition, were there not a number of extremely irritating and almost preposterous "riders" attached to these national requirements by the local extremist administration. The total number of regulations in Fukien province has grown to seventeen, and school administrators quite naturally wonder how many more may be saddled upon them if they quiescently accept without protest restrictions which in effect will choke off religious liberty and academic freedom.

Our going to Foochow was of the greatest significance for the Christian community just at this point. We were able on several occasions to show them that there were far larger issues confronting them than whether or not the Christian schools should register. They must make sure that in the principles of this new nationalist government the right of private education is maintained, that religious liberty is guaranteed, that academic freedom is not denied, and that the government actually became what it purported to be, representative of the people.

The number of junks and house-boats in the river increased; launches and tugs dodged here and there in the traffic, the smell of fish and river shipping became more acute, the houses at the water front crowded upon each other taking up every available foot of light and space: we had arrived at Foochow. Up the river a short distance from our landing place on Nan Tai stretched the stone spans of the picturesque bridge of Ten Thousand Ages, uniting the land on which we were disembarking with the mainland and Foochow. Traffic was too thick for us to get to the dock itself; we tied up as close as we could, and still had to clamber over two good-sized native boats to get

---

* For full text of registration conditions pertaining in Fukien in April, 1927, see Exhibit B, page 38.

to terra firma. Then through the narrow streets of a native bazaar at the water front, up a series of stone steps to the high ridge of the island where the principal foreign residences and institutions are located. Most of the men were without their wives in the missionary community, and the Wiants were practically the only ones equipped to take care of guests, so we not only took up our abode with them, but their home was used for several of the receptions and missionary gatherings held during our stay. The weather was cool and delightful, much like the early spring in America, a welcome contrast to the heat we had endured through Malaysia and the Philippines. The weather made a remarkable difference, for we found ourselves at once with more energy and ability to go through long hours of sustained effort.

No program that we have been asked to follow anywhere was better laid out than the one for our eight days in Foochow. It began at 8 o'clock on Friday night, April 22, the day of our arrival, with an informal conference between a few of the Chinese Christian leaders and the missionaries of the Board of Foreign Missions. At this meeting, the missionaries and Chinese proposed the major topics which they would like to have considered during our visit to Foochow, as well as specific questions they wanted answered.* Into the atmosphere of gloom and concern over their own affairs in Foochow and Fukien, we at once injected a little optimism by relating the situation we had found in India, in Malaysia, particularly Java and Sumatra, and in the Philippine Islands where people are all astir, showing signs of new life and new hope, confronting the Christian enterprise with new problems in every country, just as they are doing in China. We told them also the thrilling story of the work of the Rhenish Mission among the Battaks in North Sumatra, where, in sixty years of concentrated effort, they have transformed a population of savage cannibals into a law-abiding Christian community of churches and schools, that represents one of the most inspiring victories of Christian Missions in the whole world. It is good to remember at times that, in the face of insuperable obstacles, great things have been wrought through the Gospel of Christ in Asia, and even greater things can yet be done.

From eight to twelve on Saturday morning, we made a tour of the Christian institutions in Nan Tai. In order that we might get a bird's-eye view of the layout, we were taken to the fire tower on the top of the hill of the Fox Devil's Spirit. We saw the thirty mile long island of Nan Tai, a huge elbow in the Min River high and rocky at the point where we stood, sloping to rice fields and Chinese villages both before and behind. It was to this high and desolate eminence that the "foreign barbarians" were consigned by the arrogant Manchus in the days when the Honorable John Company was trying to extend its business from India to China. In those days there was only a small fishing village at the Nan Tai end of the bridge of Ten Thousand Ages, with other native villages in the rice growing section of the island. The foreigners took the unpromising, rocky high ground, transformed it into

---

*For complete list, see Exhibit C, page 43.

a city of pleasant streets and substantial buildings, and, today, the property is the most valuable of anything in that region. From our eminence we could see the bridge running from Nan Tai to the mainland, resting midway upon a small, thickly congested island in the river. Along the shore line on the mainland was a thickly populated section at the water front, then a narrow carriage road of high ground extending across rice fields to the old walled city of Foochow, which is still, today, the social and political center for the Chinese life of Fukien province. The White Pagoda stood out clear against the horizon, marking the right extremity of the wall, and to the left we could see the dark prominence of Black Rock Hill with the wall circling its base. Each landmark in the old city seemed to mark the site of a Christian missionary organization. Near the White Pagoda, we were told, lay Foochow College and the hospital of the American Board, and way to the north, in the shadow of the Drum Tower, just visible, the Church Missionary Society had its headquarters. Conspicuous in the foreground on the water front was the splendid four-story brick building of the Young Men's Christian Association, and not far away, the new cathedral (Chinese) of the Church of England.

We set out more closely to visit the Christian institutions on the island of Nan Tai, particularly those under the auspices of our own Church. We climbed down again through the trap-door of the fire tower, passed several small altars at the foot, dedicated to the malignant spirit of the fox-devil, with a Chinese inscription over one altar equivalent to our "Ask and it shall be given you"; scrambled among the gravestones which mark every hillside in China; and walked along the gravel path to the former headquarters of the Methodist Publishing House. The Press has been consolidated with the Interdenominational Publishing House in Shanghai long ago, and all that is left is a small stationery and office-supply store. Some of the former press rooms and offices are now the draughting rooms and headquarters for the Fukien Construction Bureau, an efficient organization with two missionary architects and engineers, and a staff of Chinese assistants who design and build not only for our own Church but for other denominations and for the general public. We visited the Church of the Heavenly Rest, built adjacent to a Buddhist monastery which bears that name, and which was famous, in 1897, when the church was erected; but the fame of the monastery is a thing of the past and the church has appropriated its lustre. There are four or five substantial missionary residences on the compound of the Board of Foreign Missions adjacent to the church. On our way to the Anglo-Chinese College we passed the stone structure of the Church of England. Anglo-Chinese College, the pioneer of English education for the whole of China, has long outgrown its old quarters. Three beautiful new buildings have been erected on one of the highest spots on Nan Tai, and they stand out clearly against the horizon as a substantial tribute to Christian education. In former days, boys came to this institution from many parts of China, and from Chinese communities in Malaysia, the Philippines and Burma. With its primary and middle schools, it is a first-class preparatory school, fitting boys to enter Fukien Christian University.

Hwa Nan (South China) College is the girls' institution of collegiate grade, maintained by the Woman's Foreign Missionary Society, just across the road from Anglo-Chinese College. At Hwa Nan, under the leadership of Dr. Ida Belle Lewis, the foreign and Chinese staff are graduating an unusually high type of Chinese young women. It was interesting to find that nearly every member of the staff, including the president, wears her hair bobbed, and a number of the Chinese girls have followed suit. We stopped, also, at the Union Bible Training School, and at the Woolston Memorial Hospital of the Woman's Foreign Missionary Society, closed for lack of a doctor.

Immediately after lunch, we met the staff of the Anglo-Chinese College, chiefly Chinese, to hear them speak frankly on the question of registration. It was evident from the many angles at which the subject was presented, that these men were unanimous in their desire to have the college register, and some of them were pretty outspoken in their demands that the Church in America relinquish control, but continue to support its educational institutions in China. That evening, there was another gathering at the Wiant home, this time including the entire foreign staffs of the Board and the Society in Foochow.

On Sunday morning, there was a conference with the men on the subject of personnel in the Mission, concerning the future place of the missionary, especially in terms of the actual need of the field. At its close, we were taken to one of the smaller Chinese churches on Nan Tai and returned in time to hear the sermon of Pastor Ding and participate in the annual thank-offering of the Chinese Woman's Home Missionary Society. They put it across with the enthusiasm of women the world over, and counted over four hundred dollars (Mex) into the coffers of their Society for work in other parts of China. This was in the Church of the Heavenly Rest, known in Chinese as Tieng Ang Dong. Sunday evening, and in fact every spare hour, was filled by conferences with individual missionaries and Chinese Christian leaders.

An outstanding impression of our work in Foochow, and one that offers great promise for the future, is the high quality of Chinese leadership. In the Foochow Conference, there are several men who have taken their M.A. degrees in the best schools in America. Two of them are preachers of outstanding ability, and perhaps half a dozen, both men and women, are teachers in our Christian schools. The high places they hold and the devotion they are giving to the Church in no small measure are due to the willingness of the foreign staff to stand aside and place responsibility upon the Chinese leaders. The fellowship among the missionaries, and between the two racial groups is truly an inspiration. Foochow is our earliest station in China, and for seventy-five years concentrated work has been done over a limited area. The density of the Christian population in Fukien is greater than anywhere else in China.

On Monday morning, April 25, we had breakfast at the Middle

School for Chinese girls, of which Miss Florence Plumb is principal. She told us of the remarkable changes in Chinese womanhood during the past twenty-six years. The entire morning was given up to chapel addresses in our various schools. Important interviews were had with Mr. Munson, of the Foochow Y. M. C. A., Mr. Price, the American Consul, and others.

Monday afternoon was filled with intimate personal conferences with Chinese and Americans, conferences that cannot be over-estimated for their value at getting to the heart of the prevailing state of affairs by the question and answer method. Late in the afternoon, another prolonged session was held with the missionaries of the Board on the subject of personnel, when the report of the committee was made in which the missionary staff for the next few years was realigned, so as to do with six less missionaries in the Foochow Conference, and thus bring the staff of Americans within the available budget. The men in Foochow are clearer in their own thinking about the future place of the missionary as a helper of the Chinese than we have found anywhere in our travels.

The five evenings, Monday to Friday, were filled with dinners which mark late hours well spent in memorable gatherings.

DINNER NUMBER ONE. This was held at the fine Women's Bible Training School, Nan Tai, and was attended by 120 Chinese Christian and missionary friends in honor of our visit to Foochow. It was a gala event of the first order, a Chinese feast with the proverbial nineteen courses, and excellent after-dinner speeches by the Chinese, that forever put the quietus on the Western belief that the Chinese have no sense of humor. In the welcome address by Mr. Hu, the speaker said his first impressions of the Corresponding Secretary were of a laughing Buddha, good-natured, smiling, with big ears, and bringing with him the money bags! He had purposely offered to carry Mrs. Diffendorfer's purse on her arrival to gauge its weight; he found it quite light, but trusted it was filled with checks and money orders. Only one who has carried around a pocketful of Mexican dollars in Chinese silver, or a bag full of Chinese "cash" can appreciate the tonnage. Mrs. Diffendorfer, the speaker said, he had thought must surely be the wife of a commissioner, she looked so distinguished. He found on closer examination, however, that she was a hard-working woman, for her face was full of lines. To call one aged is the height of respect in China, but the speaker's inverted compliments in English simply made his speech all the funnier. My come-back was interpreted by the Chinese district superintendent, Rev. Wong Gang Huo, an M. A. from Cornell College, and it was a masterpiece of another sort, as he made my speech his own and kept the crowd in constant roars of laughter. As an expression of fellowship and interracial friendship, the dinner was one of the most successful we have ever attended. The keynote of the evening was the sense of deep and abiding fellowship which exists among those who are brothers in Christ, a fellowship that transcends all the barriers of nationality, race or time.

DINNER NUMBER TWO. This was held at the Hwa Nan College

on Tuesday evening, and was scheduled for seven-thirty. We sat down to the table at nine-thirty and continued to sit until midnight. This dinner was a sacrifice upon the altar of shirt-sleeve diplomacy. The guests of honor were the military and political leaders of the Kuomintang government in Fukien Province. Principal among them was General Chang, the commander of the military forces for Fukien Province, the chairman of the Administrative Council, together with numerous smaller officers, aides-de-camp, ex-bandits, the Commissioner of Education, and gentry. Every man who had a right to military escort brought along a bodyguard, and the entrance to Hwa Nan was filled with Chinese soldiers armed to the teeth. All of the talk was through interpreters, with most of the arrangements cared for by the Hwa Nan staff and some of our Chinese Christians. As an occasion for breaking down unfriendliness and suspicion between the government and the Christian community in Foochow, it was memorable, and a lot of water was poured on the Christian wheel despite the strain of the evening's proceedings. They kept faith with their party training and lectured us at length on the three principles of Sun Yat Sen, national unity, economic reconstruction, and democratic government. Our side replied by reminding the government that it should guarantee religious freedom, academic freedom, and the safety of life and property. We were assured, in terms that made everybody happy, that the government intended to do all these things, but at the present time was hampered in doing so by the presence of a radical element with whom they found it difficult at times to cope. Good feeling predominated, and at the close of the evening, the general arose in a burst of enthusiasm and invited us all to come to dinner as his guests the following night at the Y. M. C. A.!

DINNER NUMBER THREE. The return engagement was as big a hit as the dinner at Hwa Nan. There were more of us present, including one more of "them," the number one man of the entire Fukien government, so far as a commission form of government can have a number one man, the chairman of the Political Council. It wasn't so much of a strain as the evening before; we seemed to be old friends.

There was a great crowd of us present; a number of other missionaries had taken advantage of the general's all inclusive invitation, and the total group at the Y. M. C. A. must have numbered fifty people. We were the center of attraction, also, for a crowd of onlookers, both civilians and military, who stood around in the "Y" halls frankly curious about all the hilarity. After the chairman had made his address of welcome, stressing the desire of the new government for friendship between the United States and China, and lecturing us further on the three principles of Dr. Sun Yat Sen, and we had replied, the opportunity was given for any to speak who wanted to—a sort of Methodist testimony meeting. Dr. Ida Belle Lewis, daughter of the late Bishop Lewis, and now president of the Hwa Nan College, was the first to put in her testimony for friendliness to China. Lucy Wong, one of the teachers at Hwa Nan, an up-to-date young Chinese with an American education, arose and said that she was a graduate of Hwa Nan

College, and a Christian. She and her students believed in the principles of the Kuomintang, but they objected to having the Bible taken out of the curriculum. It was a straight from the shoulder speech in Mandarin, and must have struck the new government a bit queer, coming from a woman, so rarely heard in the life of China in the past, and from one whose life had been in jeopardy many times in recent weeks. Ralph Ward felt called upon to liven things a bit, so he arose to suggest that all the visitors arise and sing to the time-honored tune, "Glory, Glory, Hallelujah, the Kuomintang Is Here!" Not to be outdone, the chairman of the Political Council arose and led all the Chinese in a Chinese yell, "Long live America! Yea! Long live China! Yea! Long live the Kuomintang! Yea!"

When we left, late at night, and a knot of us assembled at the foot of the Bridge of Ten Thousand Ages, the young Chinese who had acted as the go-between in making arrangements for the dinner, David Hung, another American graduate, said to us, "In their speeches they said the Kuomintang was bringing to the people of China national unity, food to eat, work to do; all of them material needs. The spiritual need they cannot meet; it remains for us as Christians to fill that need."

DINNER NUMBER FOUR. On a hill higher than all the hills in Nan Tai perches a group of buildings known as Miss Lambert's School. Miss Lambert is an English missionary, an unusual person who has been in China thirty-eight years, and has passed unruffled through twenty or more revolutions and the counter-marching of armies for a quarter of a century, quietly conducting her girls' school, turning back a stream of educated women into the Chinese community. Her home was the center, on Thursday evening, of a dinner given by the Fukien Christian Federation, which is the provincial branch of the National Christian Council. The chairman of the Federation is a capable Chinese man, concerning whom Bishop Hind, of the Church of England, said as we were walking home together, "I'm going to try to have him elected bishop at the diocesan meeting next week." A precise young Chinese, graduate of Syracuse, who interpreted in beautiful English, was pointed out to us as the young Church of England chaplain who had been stripped of most of his clothes, crowned with a dunce cap, and paraded through the streets of Foochow as a running dog of the imperialists by a group of hot-headed students and teachers who were demanding the immediate turning over of Mission schools to government. The Sunday after that incident happened, he went into his pulpit and preached with more directness and fire than ever before, and to the biggest congregation he ever had.

The most wonderful thing that is happening in China today is these incidents of loyalty and suffering on the part of Chinese Christians. They, and not the foreigners, are bearing the real brunt of the anti-Christian movement in China, for there are few among them who can flee to the foreign concessions for protection. Another outstanding personality in this gathering was our own Methodist, Mr. Hu Ing Huan, who is executive secretary of the Fukien Christian Federation. One of our missionaries in referring to him said he was more like an efficient American secretarial executive than any other Chinese he knew.

Into this group of upstanding, self-reliant Chinese leaders was projected the voice of self-relinquishment from a man of gray hairs, who had given his life to China. Dr. Beard, of the American Board in Foochow, arose to bid good-bye to his colleagues, announcing to them that as a result of the actions taken in conference just a few days previous, the American Board Mission in Foochow had been dissolved into the United Christian Church of South China, and that at the close of his furlough, if he were to return to China, it would be at the invitation of the Church in China, and not at the behest of the Board in America. There were smiles of appreciation on the faces of the Chinese in our group. The day has come when they are willing, and in many cases ready, to assume a large share of the responsibility for the direction of the Christian movement in China. It is an inspiration to see a man like Dr. Beard, who has given his life in order that that day might come, willingly step aside and let his mantle fall upon another, and, better still, to say that he is willing to carry on as guide, philosopher, and friend to the Christian Church in China, if it wishes to have him. One saw symbolized in Dr. Beard that night at Miss Lambert's one of the aims of the modern missionary movement.

DINNER NUMBER FIVE. We officially "left" Foochow on Friday morning, bade good-bye to all the friends, and amid a burst of Chinese fire-crackers were off in a launch down river to spend the day with Dr. John Gowdy at Fukien Christian University, half way to Pagoda Anchorage. We got there shortly before noon, and the students were assembled for the weekly University convocation. We had been advertised on several posters which the boys had put up in the halls as "A Secretary of the Board of Foreign Missions, who favors registration." Apparently our attitude as it had been expressed at Foochow on the matter of the registration of Christian schools had preceded us. As it happened nothing was said to the men in conversation on the subject of registration, the word was not even used. The students were given a straight talk on the kind of leadership which China needed for the new day, and were called upon, as college men, to prepare themselves to meet the country's needs. That evening at Dr. Gowdy's home, the entire senior class was in to dinner, about ten or a dozen boys, and we got a vivid "cross-section" of the mind of the Chinese student. The question was asked as to what each was going to do upon graduation, and when none was planning to enter the ministry, some one asked, "Why not?" That precipitated a deluge of criticism upon all existing institutions, with apparently only one solution: Chinese nationalism—with a more or less serious feeling among the men, that they could serve China better through the present-day political movement than in any other way. It was certainly illuminating, if superficial.

We left about nine o'clock that evening, in a launch with a crowd who had come down by surprise from Foochow, and took up our cabin space in the heavily laden and congested Japanese packet, Fukuken Maru, headed for Shanghai.

In Shanghai

Our first day in Shanghai was given to Bishop Brown and the missionaries of the Foochow area, who had been evacuated to Shanghai. (See Exhibit D, page 43.) The next day was given to conferences with the Central and West China missionaries, especially for the study of the problems of missionary personnel. On the third day we began our formal conferences with the entire group, with an agenda which was the result of our discussions of the two days previous. (See Exhibit E, page 44.)

A Findings Committee put into form the results of our discussions. The statement, Exhibit F, page 45, was finally adopted by the entire group on the forenoon of the day of our departure from Shanghai.

In addition to these formal conferences, every other minute of our time in Shanghai was given to interviews with the leaders of the National Christian Council, both foreigners and Chinese, the Young Women's Christian Association, the Young Men's Christian Association, and with missionaries of other denominations. An interview was also held with Mr. Sterling Fessenden, Chairman of the Shanghai Municipal Council. While it was understood that stenographic notes were made of his version of the defense of Shanghai (see Exhibit G, page 49), it needs to be said, in all fairness, that Mr. Fessenden has had no opportunity to read the statement. We also interviewed Mr. J. B. Powell, editor of The China Weekly Review, whose knowledge of Chinese affairs is broad and accurate, and whose judgments are independent, liberal, and constructive. A statement by Putnam Weale at a noonday luncheon of the American Women's Club was an appeal for armed intervention. He tried to secure the sympathetic help of the club women of America to influence public opinion in the United States to support his policy for armed intervention in China.

It must be remembered that there had passed through Shanghai missionaries from the Yangtze valley on their way to Korea, Japan, and America, and it was estimated that there were at that time 1,500 missionaries temporarily in Shanghai. This group included not only those from West China who had come out early in the year, but also those from the Kiangsi Conference, and later the group from Nanking. Some of those in Shanghai had passed through difficult experiences at the hands of the military and unfriendly civilians in the interior. Their immediate interest was in the stations left behind, and the status of their work. Their attention was being given to the reports coming through by messenger, by belated mail, or by telegram of the military occupancy of this, that, or the other station, the closing of schools, the personal experiences and dangers of the Chinese Christians. It was very apparent that the missionaries in Shanghai were too close to the experiences of the previous weeks to be able to think into the future, and to realize fully the significance of present events for the Christian movement. Naturally, it was a group that was confused, somewhat discouraged, although many were able to look upon their experiences as incidents in the larger movements manifesting themselves now in the Chinese revolution. A great assembly of the missionaries was held in Shanghai each week. On May 4, in Martyrs' Hall, the meeting was addressed by Dr. Henry T. Hodgkin, a secretary of the National Christian Council of China, on *Prophets and the Purpose of God*. The statement seemed so significant for the occasion and audience that a digest is reprinted from stenographic notes as Exhibit H, page 51.

Later, Dr. C. Y. Cheng, a secretarial colleague of Dr. Hodgkin in the National Christian Council, addressed the group in Martyrs' Hall on *Some Problems Confronting the Christian Movement in China*. This address clearly sums up the attitude of the ablest Chinese Christians on the bearing of the present events in China on the Christian movement. The full text is found on page 53 as Exhibit I.

In Peking

After a day in Tientsin, spent largely in studying our property situation, we went to Peking and began a series of conferences with missionaries and Chinese leaders from West China, and the Shantung and North China Conferences.

At the time of our visit, North China was just being threatened by a serious northern advance of the nationalist armies. In the North China Conference, a staggering financial situation confronted us which would have been a live issue in normal times, but which was accentuated by the possibility of the North going through some of the same experiences as the rest of China. Most of our time in Peking was given to this most perplexing question. The treasurer's statement showed that the Conference was in debt over $500,000 Mex. Some of this was on the missionary budget, a part consisted of accumulated deficits on the work budget for the last fifteen years, a large item was on the East City property, taken by us in our adjustment with Peking University.

This discussion brought out the further fact that the educational endowment funds of the North China Conference had been invested in Peking real estate, and were already showing signs of uncertain income.

We conferred two days with Bishop Grose and the North China missionaries of the Board on these financial problems, and had a day or more of conference with all the missionaries, including the Woman's Foreign Missionary Society representatives. on some of the more general problems. The docket for these discussions is found in Exhibit J, page 62, and shows what the group considered to be of the most importance among the issues which we face in North China today. It will be observed that there is a striking similarity to the problems in other parts of China, even though the approach and the circumstances were somewhat different. Two days were given to a meeting of the regular Field Finance Committee, of which a majority is Chinese. We also saw the first meeting which had ever been held in North China between the Field Reference Committee of the Woman's Foreign Missionary Society, and the Field Finance Committee of the Board of For-

THE SITUATION IN CHINA

eign Missions. This joint conference was found necessary in view of the common problems which the Board and the Society are now facing in regard to personnel, property and relations to the Chinese.

In addition to these formal conferences on our own problems, we were able, in Peking, to spend a day at Yenching University, and later to meet the University's committee on re-organization growing out of the demands for registration and the nationalistic sentiment. We interviewed United States Minister MacMurray, Dr. C. C. Wong, who is Postmaster-General of the Peking Government and one of our most prominent Methodist laymen, and Dr. W. W. Yen, formerly the Prime Minister of the Peking Government. We attended a luncheon at Dr. Koo's residence, the house in which Sun Yat Sen died during his visit to Peking, in 1925, where we met a number of distinguished guests and foreign visitors, including Dr. Manley O. Hudson, of Harvard University; Mr. S. Padoux, French Adviser to the Peking Government; Dr. Y. W. Kwo, professor of law at Yenching University; Mr. Frank B. Riley, of the London Times; Dr. Lo Wen Kan, Minister of Justice; Dr. Lucius Porter, of Yenching University; Dr. R. O. Bevan, and Bishop Grose.

There was time also for interviews with the secretaries of the Young Men's Christian Association and missionary leaders of other denominations; for a special luncheon with representative Chinese in the city; for addresses to the students of the Peking Theological Seminary, the Academy, the Mary Porter Gamewell school; and for many hours spent in private conference with Bishop Grose.

CHINA'S REAL REVOLUTION

As we left China on a three-day sea voyage to Japan we thought and prayed over these experiences and have written down the impressions of the momentous events that are not only shaking China, but producing rumbles in every country in the Far East.

The first and foremost fact is the reality of the revolution.

The forces operating among the Chinese are striving after nationhood, which is more pro-Chinese than anti-foreign; the desire for national unity; aspiration for complete political autonomy; the desire for equality among the nations; a sense of unfair treatment of China from the Treaty Powers; a desire to be rid of the fighting war lord factions; and the belief in a great future for China, which amounts almost to a religious fervor.

These forces are producing profound changes in China's social structure, her economic life, her educational procedure, and her political organization.

In her social life, the family system, with obedience from the sons demanded by the father, and from the wives by the mother-in-law, is beginning to give way to the independent family unit. The concubine system, which probably grew out of the traditional desire for a son in every family, will slowly disappear. Pre-arranged marriages, with no acquaintance, courtship and consent between the bride and bridegroom are giving way to love making on the part of youth, although the pro-Chinese spirit of the present is still retaining the gorgeous wedding processions, presents, and feasts. One of the most noticeable aspects of the new social life is the freedom, initiative, and independence of the new Chinese woman. There are the beginnings today in China of a real feminist movement.

Economically, the biggest factor is the coming of modern industry and the replacing of the old labor guilds and apprentice system by modern, organized labor unions. The organization of peasants' unions is scattering discontent throughout the agricultural regions. The urge for economic reconstruction lies in the desperate poverty of the masses of the people, with all forms of labor underpaid. Food, clothing, and shelter are the demands of these millions.

In educational circles, there is an almost universal conviction that the Chinese must control the schools in China, with curriculum and methods of instruction adapted to the needs of Chinese life: a movement that finds expression in various demands for the legal registration of schools, with more or less stringent regulations added by national, provincial, and local governments.

Politically, there is widespread dissatisfaction with one-man or autocratic government, whether it be by a benevolent emperor or by a rapacious and decapitating war lord. There is also recognition that the country is not ready for the exercise of the full franchise, which lies at the basis of all popular, democratic government. The nationalist government, therefore, has developed a commission form of government, in which the political council is the highest official body in the nation, in the province, the county, and the municipality. The chairman of this council would correspond to our president, governor, mayor or alderman. Each commissioner on these councils is responsible for a certain department of government, and may have a commission of his own made up of the members of sub-departments under him. There is an attempt to make a budget, to pay ordinary salaries, and to collect and disperse taxes for the common welfare, the results of which are apparent particularly in Canton and the Kwangtung Province.

Whether in the conservative north, or in radical Hankow, or in moderate Nanking, or Canton, as affecting the military situation, the revolutionary factors just mentioned have deep hold upon the majority of thinking Chinese. They have taken root among the students of China, especially the returned students, among the laboring men, and more recently among the farmers.

While the revolution of 1911, arising in the south under the leadership of Sun Yat Sen, was directed particularly against the old Manchu regime, its more positive side had its basis in the three principles which are now animating the Kuomintang, namely, national unity, economic independence, and democratic government. The present revolution in China is different from all those that have preceded it in Chinese history. A statement, agreed to by practically every one with whom we discussed the subject, is that the basis of the present nationalist uprising does not rest upon the victories of contending factions and rival war lords, but in a political and social doctrine. Every recruiting camp and every training school and officers' training college, and every army is a school for the study of these political doctrines and their relation to the future of China. Quantities of literature have been printed, and a party organization has been outlined with the minutest detail. After the contending armies of the nationalist movement have passed through a province, there follows, immediately, a political organization set up on the new lines, each member of which has had his training in the principles of Kuomintang. As we have heard these men give their greetings, present their compliments, send messages to America, and justify their position among their own people, we have observed an almost naive and simple trust in what this new doctrine will do for the reconstruction of China. This is at once the strength of the revolution and its weakness. It is our judgment that whatever the success of the various contending factions now in China, the more fundamental revolution in China will go on, probably with success and possibly here and there with dismal failure, especially if China's economic resources continue to be destroyed through the devastations of warring factions.

The hopeful factor in the revolution, as viewed from without, is the deep conviction on the part of influential, well-to-do, well educated Chinese in all parts of China that the revolution cannot and must not fail.

From the Chinese point of view, which in the last analysis is the point of view we have to reckon with, the revolution seems to me to consist in this:—The Chinese are a people with a strong sense of their own inherent worth, coming down through the years from the philosophy of the Middle Kingdom, a people "Exalted to Heaven," with an ethical code exalting "the superior man," which has been the bulwark of Chinese unity as against foreign aggression of every kind, for centuries and centuries.

Along with this tradition, is the culture of the superior man almost exclusively within the simple family circle, a series of social relationships which have been perfected and taught and accepted for generations, without question. Suddenly, through contacts with the modern world, these people have come to see that their country was gradually being penetrated by foreign commerce and business protected by foreign governments, with her modern education fostered by almost every nation of the world and in almost every language of the world—Japanese, German, Norwegian, English, Italian, French, some of the schools having a foreign language as their medium of instruction—her new religion expressed in churches and institutions of foreign origin, not only the denominational but often the individual buildings having foreign names.

These people, finding their training in the simple social life of the family and the clan, with no organization comparable to their modern educational, social, commercial, and religious contacts, have finally determined that their social organization must be revamped, their economic life reconstructed, their political unity established, their traditions as a peaceful people without an army set aside, in order that they may come into full nationhood, respected by the rest of the world.

One of the tragic things in the history of the Far East is the fact that when the United States, Great Britain, and France, with their traditional love of freedom, independence, and democracy, had an opportunity to strengthen the nationalist movement in China during its early days, through recognition, friendly contacts, advice, education in political organization, methods of popular education and propaganda, as well as in finance—a small price to pay for the attainment of a self-conscious sister nation on the other side of the Pacific—a deaf ear was turned. It was then that the Chinese leaders turned toward Russia, to a people who had liberated themselves from the worst absolutist government that the modern world has ever known. The thread of sympathy, slender enough at first, was strengthened and twisted into a cord which was at once mutually helpful, but which may become for China a strangling noose. The Russians were evidently eager enough to extend a helping hand, for it gave them much needed opportunity for commercial expansion. The Chinese, on the other hand, gained political prestige and technical organization.

On the much mooted question as to the extent and effectiveness of Russian influence in China, little is gained by over-estimating it on the one hand, or by belittling it on the other. Russia was wise enough to take advantage of the China situation at the right moment. The Russians won the confidence of the people of China in 1923 when they formally gave up their extra-territorial rights in China and accepted China as an equal among the nations. Russia withdrew her minister from China and sent a full fledged ambassador, with one stroke winning the gratitude of China and placing the Russian legation at the head of all other legations in Peking. Russian military officers brought discipline, modern tactics, organization, and strategy to the Chinese armies. Russian political advisers brought party organization and produced an effective method for securing loyalty to the principles of Kuomintang.

The Kuomintang, started by Dr. Sun forty years ago, has been the most active military and political agency in the development of the revolution. Kuomintang principles are at the heart of the Nationalist movement, whether actually admitted or not, in every section of China. Today, one joins Kuomintang by answering a series of questions on an application blank, which is sent to party headquarters, and, when accepted, a membership card is given. (See Exhibit K, page 64.)

Local party groups are then formed for the securing of new members, for the education of members in the party principles, and for carrying out such purposes for the development of the party as may be agreed upon. Kuomintang groups are found in our schools and hospitals, among students, servants, and staffs, in our churches, among both laymen and preachers, in labor unions, among farmers, and among ricksha coolies.

Russia, no doubt, was responsible for the plan of party education in the schools, including instruction in party principles, and the weekly observance of the Sun Yat Sen memorial. The latter is one of those strokes of genius for the visualizing of a great movement around an individual, a factor in all democratic countries. All will agree that it was Russia who furnished the technique, the method, the writers, and the organization of nationalist propaganda, both in China and abroad, probably the greatest exhibition of propaganda in the modern world since the Great War. From Russia also came hundreds of thousands of rubles for the definite support of army officials, political leaders, and propagandists.

It is not surprising, therefore, that the extremists, the radical communists, should take advantage of this extraordinary opportunity for the promulgation of their own doctrines in a market that was wide open. That this was done, there is evidence sufficient and complete. Gradually there appeared in this great patriotic movement the pernicious doctrine of class conflict, anti-religious sentiment, with the introduction of the principle of the destruction of the existing economic order, with its slogans of "Down with imperialism," "Down with capitalism," "Down with the foreigners," "Down with religion," "Down with the missionary," carried far and wide in pamphlets, books, newspapers, bulletins, and posters, making an effort to break down Chinese traditional social organization, the sanctity of her family life, the modesty of her womanhood, and the traditional friendliness between employers and employees.

In striking contrast to Russia's position stands the attitude of the Great Powers toward China. Granting a long list of manifest provocations, failures, and weaknesses which the world well knows, it must be admitted that the so-called Treaty Powers, consciously or unconsciously, were, from the beginning, out of an age of exploration, discovery, colonization, the establishment of trade and dominion, heading straight into a policy for the partition of China, and, having failed in that, the establishment of spheres of influences, and, failing in that, of peaceful penetration of a resourceful country with a peaceable people, unacquainted through centuries of preferred isolation with the ways of Western nations. In these adjustments, all sorts of peculiar provisions have been made, such as concessions, settlements, extra-territorial privileges, unilateral treaties, and the foreign control of customs and salt revenues. It may well be argued that these special arrangements were found necessary in dealing with a people of China's traditions and lack of experience in modern political and commercial life. This, however, does not modify or lessen the effect which this treatment has had upon China. This latter fact needs now to be taken into account. These policies, when backed up by force displayed through the years among a peaceable people, without modern armies for the protection of properties and human lives, have furnished the soil in which the seeds of the revolution were planted.

And more recently, the demands from both within and without China for the Powers to adopt a strong policy of armed intervention are furnishing today the surest weapons for the radical propagandist. We, Westerners, may justify such policies in all good conscience, believing that they may be the best thing for China, but we ought not to blink at the plain facts of the effect they are having upon the Chinese, themselves. The educated Chinese know perfectly well that all over the world, commerce, science, and religion run tremendous risks among unstable governments, savage peoples, warring factions, and racial or national prejudices. They ask the simple question, "Why do the foreigners stay here?" Again, it may well be argued that such a question is naive and does not take into account the interdependence of the modern world, and the inevitable mingling of the people of the world in commerce, education, and culture. But such a feeling on our part does not modify the views which the Chinese are now taking of the matter, and it is these attitudes and sets of mind and points of view and inner convictions among the Chinese that constitute for us the greatest factors in the present situation.

WHAT DOES THE PRESENT SITUATION MEAN FOR THE CHRISTIAN MOVEMENT IN CHINA?

I. Missionary Personnel

This question is raised, not with the hope that any final answer can be given or ought to be attempted. The outcome of the present tendencies in China is so uncertain that it is probably a truism to say that we can do little or nothing more than to think through our problems as they arise, meeting the issues from time to time. This uncertainty of the future, however, should not prevent us from recording our judgment and taking such actions as are clear at the present time. Indeed, only in such a process will we be able, at this distance, to keep abreast of the rapidly moving events which are modifying so fundamentally the social and political structure of China.

The Board of Foreign Missions last year appropriated $475,565 for China. Of this amount $296,905 is for the missionary budget, which includes the salaries, allowances, furlough travel, medical costs, itinerating and other expenses, of 332 missionaries, the number in China when these appropriations were made in November, 1926. From the total amount, $178,660 is the work budget, which is used for our schools, hospitals, and the salaries or part salaries of Chinese district superintendents, ministers, evangelists, and other workers. During the year 1926, the Chinese themselves gave for all purposes $87,096. Last year, 22 per cent of our total appropriations went to China. It will be recalled when our reduced income of 1924 compelled a reduction of one fourth of our appropriations that the missionaries and the Chinese in China, by desperate and heroic measures of self-sacrifice, endeavored to provide for their work without very materially reducing the personnel. Thus, they did not make the readjustment in personnel which occurred in other fields, a fact which must be taken into account as we consider the future of our missionary program.

As we face up to our future missionary policy in China, the following facts must be kept in mind.

1. At the present time, 115 of the missionaries in active service in China last year when our appropriations were made are now in America; 11 are in nearby countries; 22 are in Shanghai; and as far as we know, 68 are at their stations. This so-called evacuation presents many problems. Probably the time has not yet come when the wisdom or the unwisdom of the evacuation order can be justly reviewed. There is certainly a diversity of opinion regarding it among missionaries, business men, and consular agents. Minister MacMurray, in Peking, anticipated many criticisms and recriminations with reference to the general evacuation, but was himself clear in his justification of the step, even though the impression which he left upon me as to the motives behind the order is not at all clear. Consul Price, in Foochow, who had one of the most difficult situations to face, is the son of a missionary from Burma, is a deeply spiritual man, and is not only sympathetic but openly supports the missionary program, and sees in the rapid extension of the Christian movement of a definite evangelistic sort the only hope for the future of China. Mr. Price has filed with me a carefully prepared statement of the policy of our government as he understood it and attempted to carry it out in the Consular District under his care. (See Exhibit L, page 65.)

It is interesting to observe that when the United States destroyer was driving full speed ahead to Manila, with a group of frantic and terrified men, women, and children from Foochow, the British Consul in Foochow was distressed almost to obstinacy over the order which he had received to withdraw all British subjects from the interior of Fukien province to Foochow, and himself issued the order against his own best judgment. When we arrived in Foochow, we found the British residents from the interior in the city itself, and they had remained there throughout all of the days when our American citizens were in the Philippine Islands.

Whatever may be the pros and cons of the wisdom of the evacuation order, it is the fact of the evacuation which has brought forward several very concrete issues. The first and foremost is the additional expense, including transportation, extra living costs, and in some cases medical service and clothes, and the personal necessities of living. In these items, there is not included the loss of missionary residences, the libraries and instruments, but only those additional expenses to the missionaries themselves due to the evacuation order. The situation was so desperate in Shanghai and the missionaries were raising so many questions about the attitude of the Board toward them, that a letter was written to the office of the Board asking that the Board give formal assurance to the missionaries that these additional costs would be refunded to them, and that copies of this letter be mailed to all the missionaries in China who were affected. In this letter no promise was given, knowing well that this is a matter for the Board itself to decide, but we did agree to bring the matter to your attention with all the strength at our command. We urge, therefore, that if it has not already been done the Board take some official action assuring our missionaries that these personal losses will be made good, and set in motion those processes for the determining of the items and the filing of the claims. The latter has already partially been done by Treasurer Main in Shanghai, but needs to be more systematically cared for over China as a whole.

As to the effect of the evacuation upon both the Christian and the non-Christian community in China, no action of this Board can possibly overcome the misunderstandings, the deep questionings on the part of the Chinese Christians, the sarcastic and sometimes diabolical reactions of the anti-Christian leaders, and the unsatisfied longings of our Chinese Christians for the return of those who have shared in the building up of the Christian Church in China through all these years.

2. Since so many of our missionaries are now away from their posts, naturally one of our greatest problems is the conditions under which they may return. We raise very definitely for the consideration of the Board the possibility and desirability of not returning our missionaries to China for the time being, and possibly withdrawing those who are now there, with rare exceptions. This policy is proposed aside from any bearing which safety of life and property may have upon the question. Many of our missionaries feel that this policy would prevent any complications, due to the policy of the United States government to protect its citizens and their property, and to secure indemnification in the case of loss.

In the decision of such an important issue, we must not be unduly influenced by the sentiments expressed by leaders in our Chinese Christian community who for personal and other reasons may be urging their missionary friends to return. This is only natural, but of necessity must have a very limited bearing upon the policy as a whole. It would be natural, of course, for those Chinese Christians who are dependent upon the missionaries for their financial support to be eager for their return. As bearing upon this policy, we would call to the attention of the Board a statement which the missionaries of the American Board in North China sent to the Congregational Churches in America after a meeting in Tientsin, on April 11-12, 1927. (See page 68, Exhibit M.)

3. A fact of equal significance, which our missionaries appreciate, is the spirit in which any who go back should return to their work. The evacuation established Chinese leadership in hospitals, schools, and evangelistic work. In some districts, the choosing of responsible Chinese for places of leadership was a matter of but a few hours, especially in those instances where missionaries had been far sighted and were working definitely toward this end. In other cases it was hastily done, but everywhere it is trying and proving the mettle of the Chinese to handle our Church institutions and affairs under difficult circumstances. Thus, without any credit to ourselves, Chinese leadership has been established as one of the accompaniments of the Chinese revolution. Our missionaries are keen to feel that when they return their expressed attitude toward the Chinese who are now carrying the burden of our work is even more important than all of their previous missionary experience. Whatever may be our general policy regarding the return of

missionaries to China, the missionaries themselves will certainly see to it that the gains that have been made in the sense of responsibility and leadership for the Christian movement in China among the Chinese will not only not be lost, but will be greatly strengthened and set forward toward the new day.

It is equally true that the missionaries of the future will and should go to China on such terms as the Chinese themselves desire. Already many of our missionaries feel that this is the only basis on which they will return to their posts. There may be some missionaries who, under these conditions, would feel that they could serve the Church better somewhere else than on the foreign field, in which case we should have all respect for their judgment, involving such sacrifice of their life purpose.

Missionaries who are unwilling to go to China in these days without the protection of their lives and property by American gunboats should remain in America, and the Board should refuse to send out any whose safety must depend on foreign military and naval forces. It would be better not to return a single missionary to China for a period of years than to send out a host under the old conditions.

4. Under all these conditions, what then is the place and function of the missionary in China for the future? No question was discussed more fully and freely by missionaries and Chinese in separate and joint conferences during our visit to China. These questions came first on every agenda. Several things are clear. Any attempt to determine the number, kind, and location of missionaries to China in the future from New York would set the Chinese Church back a generation. Heretofore, we have been accustomed to making our missionary program by such studies as surveys, in which the Missionary Board or a group of Boards have attempted to outline where work should be opened, what kind of work should be done, what the qualifications and training of the missionaries should be, a programizing process that has been almost perfected in its technique. Such a policy must now be abandoned by us. Through all these years, we have now raised up a group of Chinese leaders who are probably better qualified to determine these issues than even the missionaries of long experience. We must now ask our Chinese brethren how best we can serve them and help them to train their ministry, to strengthen their churches, to mark out new lines of work, and to open up new fields of endeavor. Even in those cases where, through lack of experience and knowledge, the Chinese may not see all the opportunities now open to them, our approach in such cases must be through suggestion and helpful counsel rather than through any formal programizing of our own. Under such conditions, if they desire help from us (which they will desire increasingly), we should give that help, to quote Frank Cartwright, "to the utmost limit of our resources in men and money."

Mr. Cartwright's answer to the question, "Should missionaries stay in China?" published in The Christian Advocate of June 23, 1927, was discussed by us in China at length, and it has our hearty endorsement. His answer is as follows:

"What about the future? First, within the bounds of our present Conferences. Missionary work in such regions should be left entirely to the control of the Chinese Church. If they want continued help from American preachers, we should give that help to the utmost limit of our resources in men and money. I believe that they will ask for continued missionary help as: (a) 'Liaison officers,' who, by word of mouth or by letters, interpret the Chinese Church and its needs to the constituency in America; (b) As evangelistic helpers, men and women who will assist the district superintendents, preachers, and Bible women in their difficult and rarely inspired tasks; (c) As occasional visitors; as 'experts,' if you please, men and women who will come from foreign lands after years of experience and will advise with groups of Chinese workers. However, if any Conference feels that it can get along better without the presence of the missionary, we should, with good grace and in real rejoicing, retire from that field, conscious that the missionary aim has been reached.

"But there are wide areas outside the bounds of any Methodist Conference. These areas are not only far from Methodist influences, but many are not touched by any Christian force. Can we not, should we not, as Missions go to those regions?

"It is conceded that we could go there independently and could do much good. Very likely many missionaries and some Societies will decide to do so.

"But Methodism must not do this. We can and should let the Chinese Church know that we are willing and eager to do continued pioneer missionary work, but only on their invitation. When there were no Christians in China, our spiritual forefathers came and worked against great opposition to establish a Church. But there is a Church now. It has numerical strength. Capable leaders have been developed. That Church surely should be consulted before our Board opens pioneer work in China hereafter."

5. Will the Chinese Want Us? If our experience in Japan with the independent Japan Methodist Church means anything, there will be first a period of readjustment between the missionaries and the nationals, in which the latter will take their rightful place of leadership and the missionaries will become their helpers. Then following this, a sense of increased responsibility on the part of the nationals, and a new understanding of the problems which the small and inadequate Christian group face in the evangelization of their country. Then they will turn to us for help and ask that missionaries who can fit into their situation of need be sent to them. When such urgent calls come, the churches in America will have before them one of the greatest opportunities they have ever faced, and a real test of their genuine missionary spirit.

II. The Chinese Church

It is recognized, at the outset, that there are problems and policies regarding the Church in China that belong to our general ecclesiastical leaders and agencies, and are not within the authority of the Board of Foreign Missions. On the other hand, as long as the sum of $178,-000 is being appropriated annually by this Board for the support of Chinese work, and as long as it is the definite purpose of the Board to establish in China a self-supporting, self-directing, and self-propagating Church, we, as a Board, have the right to consider whether or not we are achieving our aims, and whether or not our appropriations are being wisely used. How far then are we succeeding in building up a Chinese Church?

1. In the very nature of the case, evangelistic missionary work had to be opened up by foreigners. From the Chinese point of view, the missionary is sent from abroad, is paid from abroad, and brings with him a new message and a strange plan for the organization of a religious society. His message is new, and one of the chief problems of the missionary is to share with the Chinese those elements of Christian experience which are universal, and to divest the Gospel and the Christ from being considered the exclusive possession of the West. Thus, in a most fundamental way, the missionary enterprise is handicapped at the point of making the message of the organized society of Christians known as the Church to take hold and become what we call "indigenous."

Then, during all these years of pioneering, each missionary group has been putting up its own denominational machinery, in the process of which, probably of necessity, the Chinese accepted foreign support for positions in a foreign organization. Our goal then, inevitably, was to make this procedure efficient. As it worked out, a foreigner with a foreign plan and foreign money, himself constantly growing in his own conceptions of his task, was continually educating and inspiring the Chinese to catch up. Our query is, on such a basis, will he ever catch up?

2. Thus we find in China, today, the outward workings of a full fledged Church: bishops, General Conference delegates, Central Conference, Annual Conferences, District Conferences, district superintendents, Quarterly Conferences, committees, and general boards and officers—always reflecting in China our own attempts to perfect this organization without sufficient regard to the foundations in Chinese life and experience, and social structure, and certainly without consulting the Chinese as to whether or not such a plan gives them the best opportunity for the expression of their organized Christian life.

Inexperience, lack of training, and our own zeal and temperament possibly made necessary this particular approach to the establishing of the Christian movement in a foreign country. Certainly, we Methodists are not peculiar in this regard. We have all followed this procedure. With us as Methodists, however, the very efficiency of our organization and what we call our connectional life constitute for us a particular problem in this regard.

3. Our missionaries were constantly opening their hearts to me in personal conferences, saying that our present emphasis on making our complicated organization succeed was resulting in an unbalanced

missionary objective. They, themselves, are feeling that, as missionaries, they are giving entirely too much time to administrative matters, and some of them feel that they have lost their true missionary purpose. They are longing for some plan by which, in cooperation with and under the direction of the Chinese, they can be set free to experiment in new lines of work, to strengthen the churches, to open up new fields of endeavor.

As long as this Church organization is supported by foreign money exclusively, the Chinese, of course, will accept it. As far as I could discover, all of our district superintendents in China are Chinese, the missionaries taking the position of district missionaries. These Chinese district superintendents are practically supported by our missionary funds. They look to the Mission for their standardized salaries, and have consequently less points of contact and sense of responsibility with their Chinese churches than they might otherwise have. It may be said that this is necessary in a stage in a growing young Church, and that the time may come when the Chinese will be able to support, not only their ministry, but also their district superintendents and their bishops. When that time comes, we must be prepared to have them express their judgment as to whether they desire to spend their money for these officers. Indeed, at the present time, it is to be doubted whether the Chinese Church would have a paid district superintendency at all, if they had to support it.

4. As to Chinese bishops, all of the groups in Foochow, Shanghai, and Peking with whom this matter was discussed were unanimous that the time has come when the Church in China should have Chinese episcopal supervision. It would be fatal, however, for us to think of a Chinese bishop as a general superintendent, elected by the General Conference, and supported by foreign money. It would be equally fatal to try to unite the Chinese on one bishop for the North, the West, the South, and Central China. Chinese episcopal supervision, it is agreed by all, should begin with some modified form of the episcopacy in one or more of these limited areas, a man chosen by the Chinese themselves and supported by them with salaries and duties fixed in their own legal conferences.

In other words the beginnings of a Christian Church in a non-Christian country should be simple in organization, adapted to the genius of the people, a natural and normal expression of their own desires, and above everything else there should be plenty of allowance for such modification and natural growth as is possible among the people themselves.

5. In China, as in India, the Philippine Islands and Korea, there repeatedly came up for discussion the question of the adaptation of our Church organization so as greatly to reduce its overhead expense with a larger emphasis upon an unpaid ministry. It will be seen, at once, that such a program has a direct bearing upon our problem of self-support and upon the appropriations from this Board, for what we call the work budget. The point I desire to make here is, that it is hardly fair for us to insist that the Chinese should support an over-

head Church organization which they, themselves, had no part in forming, and it is equally clear that as long as that organization is completely financed from abroad, it will not really take hold in the life and consciousness of the Chinese people. Our problem, therefore, seems to be to permit, by General Conference action and by constitutional methods, such adaptations of our temporal economy as will give to us a Church in China that is a true expression of the genius of the Chinese people. Incidentally, probably no man in the world would have seen this more clearly and have adopted it more eagerly than John Wesley himself. The privileges that the Methodists had, when they established their organization in America in their first General Conference, ought to be as eagerly granted by us to the Methodists of other countries.

This raises the question as to the relation of our Chinese Methodism to church unity and a National Church in China, and to our international Methodism. As in India, so in China, we found that our national Christian leaders and our missionaries have not yet found their minds on this matter. In speaking to the question, we acknowledged at all times that in the last analysis the nationals would decide this matter for themselves. On the other hand, it was pointed out to them, as faithfully as possible, what was involved in the withdrawal of our foreign churches from our international organization. We also brought to their attention, that a National Church did not necessarily mean a United National Church. It was more likely to mean uniformity and a deadening conformity to the nationalist spirit, in a day when, more than ever before, we needed the international outlook, contacts, and organization. Very much depends in this matter on the attitude of the churches in America in the next few years. Lack of confidence in the future of China, withdrawal of support from our Chinese Christians at the present time, regardless of what modifications may be made in our missionary approach and in our Church organization, and especially any evidence that we are not standing by our Chinese Christians to the limit, in these days of terrible testing, will be interpreted by some Chinese as reason for strengthening the National Church movement.

III. Christian Education in China

There is no more important and no more difficult problem which we have to face in China, today, than that of our Christian schools. The day schools, the middle schools, the boarding schools, the colleges, our theological training schools, and our great union universities are all facing a new situation in education and new relationships to government. The whole issue is made very concrete around the question of registration.

We certainly must recognize the right of China to determine her own general educational policies. The aims, content of instruction, and educational methods must be her own. She has also the right to relate the education of her youth to her own national life, and to make every school a center of patriotic instruction, quite as much so as we do in America, especially among our foreign speaking peoples.

The Chinese recognize that the only hope of unifying their country lies in an educational system that is definitely Chinese, with common ideals and common goals of instruction for the country. It is well known that China's modern education began in Mission schools, in which education was conducted by American, English, Scotch, Irish, Scandinavians, Germans, French, Italians, Russians, Japanese, and possibly others. It must also be kept in mind that, for over a quarter of a century, China has been sending her most capable sons and daughters for their college and university and technical training, in numbers into the thousands, to Japan, America, England, Germany, France, and Russia. The demands for a national educational policy in China have come from this group, known in China as the "returned students."

It must also be kept in mind that the registration of schools, with government curricula and supervision, has arisen in the Chinese National Educational Association, and is not a product of Kuomintang, Russian radicalism, or the parties of the present revolution. We probably would have been required to meet this educational situation, even though the present revolution had not occurred. The Peking government has long since demanded the registration of our schools in North China, and most of them have met the situation.

To be sure, the new Nationalist Government, especially under the influence of radical elements, is taking advantage of registration to force, not only the nationalization of the schools, but also is imposing conditions which may be intended to make it impossible for private education to exist, and for Christian schools to carry on with a definite Christian purpose. It remains to be seen whether these conditions will prevail.

The Christian Church will have no difficulty in accepting Chinese leadership and administration for their schools. They will also accept patriotic education as having a rightful place in a Christian school, whether or not the form of government under which we conduct our schools is different from our own. We will also be willing to put chapel attendance, Bible study, and other methods of religious education on a voluntary basis. If our experience in India with the conscience clause, and in Japan with these limitations in registration means anything, we have nothing to fear except, possibly, some temporary embarrassment due to the present war psychology and with the present strong propaganda against religion of any kind, and especially against Christianity.

This antagonism, in our judgment, is a passing phase in China's life, just as the acute discussions on the conscience clause in India were a passing phase. In Japan, while compulsory chapel attendance is impossible in registered schools, chapel is made so attractive and is so much a part of the organized life of the school that the boys and girls take it for granted and attend almost 100 per cent.

What our Chinese Christians are standing out for, with their own government officials, is the right of private education to exist, with the principle of religious liberty fully guaranteed, and with non-interference in academic freedom assured, a struggle which by no means is yet settled, but which is an inevitable conflict and which in the end may greatly strengthen the position of the Christian schools.

The present difficulty in registration is with the continual shifting of the conditions of registration, and the multiplicity of demands and limitations due to the uncertain and unstable political situation. Our advice in China was that we should not register except under conditions which would guarantee to us the Christian purpose of our schools, guaranteeing to our Chinese Christians full religious liberty and to our schools academic freedom, but, at the same time, with unquestionable patriotic loyalty to China, with the schools properly supervised by the Chinese government. If these conditions did not exist and there was likelihood of our closing our schools, we then recommended registration in preference to closing, in order to take the chance, as registered schools, to help modify the restrictions. We kept reminding our leaders that if conditions prevailed which would make it impossible for us to keep our schools open, those conditions would arise out of a situation which would tend to drive Christian schools out of China altogether.

The problems of our schools in China are not confined to those of registration and government supervision. If Christian education is to be maintained, it must be upon the basis that the best education possible is given in an atmosphere thoroughly Christian, and with definite Bible instruction and Christian training. In order to do this our schools can no longer be left to the uncertainties of annual appropriations from a fluctuating income. This problem is particularly acute with our middle schools. No subject was more thoroughly considered in our conference in Shanghai than the desperate need of our middle schools, and in the findings of that conference there are definite recommendations.

Here is one of the greatest challenges that we have to our Church in America, where there is now a deeper appreciation of our Church schools and a greater willingness to supply them with adequate buildings, equipment, and endowment than ever before in our history. The endowment of our schools in China in the sum total is too meager for mention. In America, our schools are maintained by tuition fees, the income from endowment, and by special current subscriptions, and by appropriations from the general educational funds of the Church through the Board of Education. In China, our schools are maintained on the fees and the appropriations of the Board of Foreign Missions, which appropriations are to the schools in China what the appropriations of the Board of Education are to the current expenses of the Church schools in America. This means that the schools are too large, are understaffed, are ill equipped, and have a constant fight to keep open from year to year.

This is one of our biggest missionary opportunities in China today. We should decide, which will not be difficult, which of these schools should permanently survive, and then ask the Church to provide an adequate endowment and equipment fund to enable them to serve effectively the present day, this being a necessary condition to enable the Chinese, in the future, to control and support their schools, themselves,

China's problem is only a reflection of similar situations in Japan, Korea, Malaysia, India, Africa, Latin America, and Europe.

IV. Medical Work

Aside from the problems which will arise in connection with individual hospitals, some of which are very important, it is clear that our medical work will be increasingly in the hands of Chinese superintendents and physicians.

Peking Union Medical College is probably the finest institution of its kind in the world. It is giving the Chinese a medical training and equipment second to none. The Chinese, with their aptitude for accurate scholarship, their deft and sensitive fingers and hands under perfect control, and their never ending patience, are endowed with gifts which help to make them capable surgeons and doctors.

Peking Union Medical College has a very definite policy of devolution. It provides that all professional positions shall be among the first to be turned over to the Chinese, and every foreign doctor has a definite program of training a Chinese to take his own department or work. In some cases, the time schedule is actually set so that the foreign doctor knows when his time is up and when he must give way to a capable Chinese successor, and be retained only as a helper under Chinese supervision. The next step is to turn over the administrative work to the Chinese, and in this there is the same program. The last stage in devolution is the turning over of the financial support of the institution. One is impressed at Peking Union Medical College by the fact that this program is all understood definitely, is planned for, and is being gradually realized. I asked one of our own cooperating physicians who is soon to go on furlough, whether he would be returning to Peking Union Medical College. He said he was not sure, but he had been invited back for another four years, and if he came that would be as long as he could stay, for at the end of that time it was expected that he would have a thoroughly equipped Chinese doctor to head his department, as a specialist in tuberculosis.

Since our largest medical work as a Board is in China, it will be seen that the situation which we now confront will have a direct bearing upon our sending of foreign doctors to China. No one would mean to intimate that no additional foreign doctors are needed. The Chinese, themselves, will call for such help and we should be ready to respond.

V. Property Problems

Our property problems apparently divide themselves into three groups: first, the Chinese churches and parsonages; second, institutions, educational, medical, etc.; third, missionary residences.

1. After carefully studying and discussing the policy of the Young Men's Christian Association and the Young Women's Christian Association in China, our conference groups in Foochow, Shanghai, and Peking were all unanimous in recommending that steps be taken to turn our church property over to some responsible Chinese holding body or bodies. A necessary condition, of course, is a responsible government,

under which some holding body can be incorporated or registered, to which the church property and parsonages can be deeded. The Young Men's Christian Association has a national holding body which owns all but a few local Association buildings, and some of these are now in process of being turned over. A few Y.M.C.A. buildings remain in foreign settlements or concessions, and therefore are outside the jurisdiction of a Chinese holding body. Our groups debated whether or not the Annual Conferences should be incorporated, or whether some holding body for all China should be organized. The Chinese feel the necessity for some such policy, but all agree that a plan should be found that will protect the property from any unscrupulous or unsympathetic local governments.

The general feeling is that an Executive Board, possibly the China section of the Executive Board of the Eastern Asia Central Conference, should be incorporated for the purpose of holding the property of Chinese churches and parsonages. We recommend that a commission be constituted in China, or that we petition the Central Conference of Eastern Asia to take the necessary steps to create such a holding body. It may take years to perfect the arrangements, but it is none too early to begin this important step. We will need to remind ourselves that it is just as important for the property which the Chinese, themselves, will own and maintain in the future, as it is for the property which has been purchased and maintained by the Board's appropriations and whose titles are now in our name.

2. As to educational institutions and hospitals, it seems clear, that in ways which the new registration laws will demand, each institution must be considered by itself, and that probably Chinese boards of managers must be created with whom the Board of Foreign Missions and Boards of Trustees in America can negotiate for any properties involved.

3. It would seem wise for us to treat separately the missionary residences and compounds. In every missionary center, sometimes on the very best possible building locations, we have large foreign residences for our missionaries, which will be of doubtful value to the Chinese in the future. Most notable of all is the large, much discussed compound in Peking, which already is furnishing a difficult problem with which to deal. As long as the Board is responsible for sending and keeping missionaries in China, these residences are the responsibility of the Board. If missionaries are no longer needed in any centers and are transferred to other centers, we should be perfectly free to transfer with them their residences.

Some of the missionary residences are very large. Most of them are in excellent condition. They were built in the days when a few thousand dollars would erect and furnish a house costing from five to ten times that sum in America. Some of them are a burden to our missionaries to maintain, and we may have requests to make over some of the residences into duplex houses, or first and second floor apartments.

4. It is agreed by all that now is no time for any building opera-

tions of any sort in China, but, rather, a time of careful conservation of all of our property interests, and of study for its wise use and care.

5. The acute financial situation in a number of our Annual Conferences will lead to some very definite recommendations for the disposal of certain pieces of property, in order to write off these obligations, and further aid the current budget through savings in interest on accumulated deficits. Our ability to negotiate such transactions will depend in a measure on political conditions, but there are situations where these conditions are not factors where we should give consideration to the definite proposals, as they are presented.

6. One of the most important property problems which the Board needs to consider is our policy with reference to Board property looted, stolen, and destroyed in the process of present war conditions. On the advice of the Embassy in Peking, the American consuls in China are asking all Americans to file statements of all losses due to these causes. This is being done as rapidly as possible. The Board must decide whether or not it will seek indemnity from the Chinese for such property destroyed. If any responsible Chinese government offers to restore such property that is one possibility. It is quite a different policy for our Board to file its claims and be included in the demands which our government may make upon the Chinese for the restitution of destroyed property. Already, other Christian groups in China have openly declared that they will not accept such indemnity, and we understand that the International Committee of the Young Men's Christian Association has sent formal notice to the State Department in Washington, and through them to the American Minister in Peking, that they would not ask indemnity for any destroyed Y.M.C.A. property in China. Our recommendation is that this Board now send official word to the State Department that we will ask no property indemnities.

VI. Standing the Test

This is the day of the Christian movement in China. The Chinese Church is being tried as by fire, is being purged and is standing the test. The strength of the foundations of the years is now being revealed. "The foundation is laid, namely Jesus Christ, and no one can lay any other. On that foundation any one may build gold, silver, precious stones, wood, hay, or straw, but in every case the nature of his work will come out." Those few who have looked upon material things —property, buildings, equipment, organization, statistics and the like— as the outward signs of Christian triumphs, may find themselves perplexed, discouraged and possibly disillusioned, but the hosts who have been planning, working, praying and hoping for signs of spiritual reality in Chinese Christians, for an awakening sense of responsibility and initiative in the Chinese Church and for evidences that Jesus Christ is at home in China will rejoice and be heartened. They will work and give with a new, determined purpose that Jesus Christ may become fully known to this great people.

Respectfully submitted,

At Sea, June 28 to July 12, 1927   RALPH E. DIFFENDORFER.

Exhibit "A"

INTERVIEW WITH DR. CHUN OF CANTON

"In 1911, Dr. Sun Yat Sen successfully established the Republic of China in the first revolution. At that time, Yuan Shai Kai was the only opposing factor in the Manchu regime. In the fall of 1911, Dr. Sun was elected provisional president of the Chinese Republic. He came to office on January 1, 1912. Yuan Shai Kai promised Dr. Sun to dethrone the Emperor of the Manchu dynasty if Dr. Sun would resign the presidency in favor of Yuan Shai Kai. Dr. Sun favored the proposition if Yuan would be true to the Republic of China. Dr. Sun resigned in favor of Yuan. Yuan took the power and made himself the Emperor of China, calling it the Yuan dynasty. He overthrew the Republic. Dr. Sun started another revolution to overthrow Yuan because he was not true to the Republic. Yuan's dynasty was destroyed in the same year by Sun's forces. All the revolutions of China have started in Canton. However, Dr. Sun did not get the supreme power. A military man controlled the northern country because he had helped Sun in the overthrow.

"Then Sun began to formulate another revolution. He sought the help of any foreign power who would come to his aid. His first approach was to the English. The British merchants of Hongkong supplied money and guns. In 1920, when Sun's forces were defeated in Canton, Great Britain changed her policy and no longer gave Sun any assistance, because they thought that Sun would never come into power again. That was the turning point in British policy. They prohibited Sun from landing in Canton. He then began to seek the help of Lenin in Soviet Russia in 1921. From that time on, Russian agents and officers were sent to China. Borodin was sent by Lenin.

"The aims of Soviet Russia in China have been first to use China as an instrument against England, and second to spread the doctrine of world revolution.

"The Kuomintang was started by Dr. Sun, 40 years ago. Soviet Russia at first limited its activities to Canton. They agitated among the laboring classes, and among the students. The common people and those with little sense were the easiest to excite. Students and laborers have been the weapons of the Kuomintang during the last few years. The Kuomintang had no army of its own in the beginning. Gen. Chiang Kai Shek, the commander-in-chief of the nationalist army, was a favorite young friend of Dr. Sun's. Chiang is only 41 years of age at the present time. After the death of Dr. Sun two years ago, he took the lead in military affairs in the Southern army. Upon the death of Dr. Sun, the Kuomintang split into the right and left wings. The left wing favors communism, and the right wing upholds the three principles of Dr. Sun Yat Sen.

"Chiang never put himself into either party. Russia helped him in his northern expedition. The left wing has divided again into moderates and extremists. The extremists stand for taking over the concessions and the custom houses by force. The moderates desire the same ends, but not by the use of force. Chiang desires to use negotiations, alone, with the Powers. The extremists had agreed that on a certain day in the month of April they would plunge into the concessions and custom houses and seize them by force. Chiang found this out and about 2 A. M. on the 14th, he captured all the extremists he could find."

As to the effect of the nationalist movement upon the Christians of China, our young friend continued:

"Two Christmases ago, they threw stones and beat their drums to interfere with our meetings. Students and laboring men did this. The nationalist movement will separate the real Christians from the unmanly

Christians. After the foreign support of the Church has been compelled to withdraw, the Chinese Christians are learning to stand on their own feet. Most of the churches in Canton have become self-supporting in the last few years.

"There is an independent South China Methodist Conference. In that Conference, are 15 churches and several missions. They use the Methodist Discipline. The Conference extends through Kwantung Province. There are about 50 Christian churches of different denominations in Canton. There is a large Roman Catholic Cathedral.

"85 per cent to 90 per cent of the Chinese people in America come from a little section of four counties in Kwantung Province, near Canton. Canton came in contact early with foreign influence. Canton is the first Chinese city to take modern ideas."

Exhibit B

REGISTRATION CONDITIONS IN FUKIEN PROVINCE

April, 1927

To Fukien Christian University:

In reply we beg to inform you that matters having to do with the registration of schools and other necessary things have been especially prepared and expressed in the form of regulations. It will be necessary for you to carry out these instructions. We now herewith send you the various kinds of regulations under separate cover. Please note and act accordingly.

From The Educational Bureau of Fukien Political Commission. Enclosures under separate cover.

A copy of the regulations for private schools.
A copy of the regulations for the establishing of the Board of Managers of private schools.
A copy of the regulations for the registration of schools.
A copy of the rules for the partynization of education.
A copy of the rules for the weekly memorial service.

April, 1927.

REGULATIONS FOR PRIVATE SCHOOLS

(Passed by the Educational Administrative Committee at its 39th meeting and promulgated on October 18, 1926.)

Art. I. The term Private School means any school that is established by private persons or any private legal body. Schools established by foreigners and churches belong to this category.

Art. II. Private schools shall be under the supervision and direction of the Educational Administrative Office.

Art. III. The name of a private school shall clearly and faithfully indicate the kind of the school. It shall be, furthermore, prefixed with two words. "Private Establishment."

Art. IV. The founders of a private school shall select persons to be organized as its Board of Managers and to have the whole responsibility for managing the school. There is a set of regulations for the establishment of the Board of Managers.

Art. V. The establishment and change of a private school shall have the permission of the Office in Charge of the Educational Administration through the petition of its Board of Managers.

Art. VI. The closing up of a private school shall be done through the petition by its Board of Managers for permission from the Administrative Office in Charge of Education. The property and other belongings of the school shall be liquidated together with Government representation.

Art. VII. The President of a private school shall be wholly (completely) responsible to its Board of Managers for the administration of the school.

Officers and teachers of the school are to be appointed and dismissed by the President.

Art. VIII. No foreigner shall be eligible for presidency of a private school. Under conditions foreigners may be engaged as advisers.

Art. IX. The organization, courses of studies, teaching schedule and other matters of a private school shall be based on the Existing Educational Ordinances.

Art. X. There shall be no required religious courses in any private school. There also shall be no religious propaganda in the classes.

Art. XI. If there shall be religious services in a private school no compulsory attendance shall be allowed.

Art. XII. The school affairs, teaching affairs, and other matters of a private school shall be reported from time to time to the Educational Administrative Office according to its orders.

Art. XIII. When a private school shall be found to be badly managed or to be in violation of ordinances the Government may dissolve it.

Art. XIV. Any private school that has not registered shall register within a time limit after the proclamation of the present regulations.

Art XV. These regulations go into effect from the date of public proclamation.

REGULATIONS FOR PRIVATE SCHOOLS FOR BOARD OF MANAGERS

(Passed by the Educational Administrative Committee at its 40th Meeting and promulgated on October 18, 1926.)

I. In a private school the Board of Managers shall represent the founders in the management of the school. The establishment of the Board of Managers must be according to the following items, to be reported by the founders to the educational administrative office for approval.

(1) Purpose.
(2) Name.
(3) Location of Board of Managers' office.
(4) Rules for the organization and power of the Board of Managers.
(5) Rules for the big meeting of the Founders and the meetings of the Board of Managers.
(6) Regulations about property, funds and other income.

In the case of middle or lower grade schools application must be made by the Board of Managers to the city or district educational bureau to be forwarded to the provincial educational office. In the case of a university or specialized college the Board of Managers shall apply through the provincial educational office to be forwarded to the national educational administrative committee. In forwarding the educational office must make investigation and send detailed comments for consideration of the national educational administrative committee. Any school which has been approved by the provincial educational office for registration must, through its Board of Managers, apply to the national educational administrative committee, by the provincial educational office, for future reference.

II. After being granted permission to establish the school according to Article I the Board of Managers shall within a month give answers to the following items to the educational administrative office of the province for registration. After permission is given for registration the answers to the following shall be filed in the office of the Board of Managers and in the local educational administrative office.

(1) Name.
(2) Location of Managers' Office.
(3) Date for permission of establishment.
(4) Detailed list of property, funds and other sources of income.
(5) Names. home addresses. professions and local addresses of members of Board of Managers.

If there are any changes in the above paragraphs 2. 4, and 5. they must be reported within seven days to the educational administrative office of the province and also to the office of the Board of Managers and to the local educational administrative office.

III. The following are the principles in regard to the power of the Board of Managers, with the exceptions permitted by the educational administrative office of the province under special conditions.

    (1) The financial responsibility of the Board of Managers.
        (a) Plan for finance.
        (b) Approval of budgeting and auditing.
        (c) Care of the property.
        (d) Supervision of finance.
        (e) Other financial affairs.
    (2) The Board of Managers will select a president for school administration with full responsibility. The board shall not have any direct participation in administration. The president-elect shall have the approval of the educational administrative office. The board may change the president when he does not meet the requirements of his position.

IV. The Board of Managers may employ officers or employees to do the work of their office according to their own rules.

V. When necessary, the educational administrative office may investigate the affairs and finances of the Board of Managers.

VI. If the school should close the Managers must report within seven days to the educational administrative office for the clearing up of the property affairs. When everything is settled a report must be made to the educational administrative office.

VII. If the school is dissolved the Board of Managers may petition the educational administrative office for permission to give the property for some other educational enterprise.

VIII. If the school is dissolved and if the property has no owner, then the educational administrative office may take it over.

IX. If there should be debts an appeal can be made to a court of justice for settlement.

X. If the Board of Managers wish to dissolve their organization, then they must appeal to the educational administrative office for permission. If their registration is withdrawn they would automatically dissolve.

XI. The Board of Managers cannot dissolve the school without the permission of the educational administrative office.

XII. The Board of Managers shall make a report within thirty days after the close of the fiscal year of the following matters, together with a list of property to the educational administrative office and to the office of the Board of Managers and to the office of the local educational administrative office.

    (1) Administrative affairs of the school.
    (2) Important events of the year.
    (3) Amount of income and expenditure, itemized.

XIII. No foreigner can be a member of the Board of Managers, but under special conditions foreigners may serve on the board, but the natives must have a majority. A foreigner cannot be chairman of the board.

XIV. These regulations will apply as soon as they are proclaimed.

REGULATIONS FOR REGISTRATION OF SCHOOLS

(Passed by the Educational Administrative Committee at its 39th Meeting and proclaimed October 18, 1926.)

1. To establish a school, with the exception of special regulations, registration must be applied for to the educational administrative office, in the case of a public school by the person in charge and in the case of a private school by the Board of Managers.

In applying for registration a school must present a petition and accompanying documents. Middle and lower grade schools with the exception of

THE SITUATION IN CHINA

schools established by the government, must apply to the city or district educational bureau, the petition to be forwarded to the provincial educational office. In case of a university and special colleges, except those nationally established, application must be through the provincial educational bureau to be forwarded to the educational administrative committee of the people's government. There must be a detailed investigation and comments forwarded with the application.

Any school whose registration has been approved by the provincial educational office must send on its petition to the national educational administration committee for reference.

2. Before applying for registration, established schools must meet the following conditions:
   (a) Funds.
       (1) There must be sufficient property or income the proceeds of which shall meet the current expenses of the school.
       (2) Or there must be some other definite source of income sufficient to meet the current expenses.
       (3) Or if there is no property or definite sources of income, then some other sources are necessary to supply enough money to meet expenses.
   (b) Equipment.
       There shall be suitable school grounds and buildings and athletic grounds and school and teaching equipment.
   (c) Teachers and officers.
       Teachers and officers must have proper qualifications. No foreigner may be the president.

3. Schools when applying for registration must answer the following questions and provide a map of the school property with explanations.
   (1) Name of school, both Chinese and foreign, if such.
   (2) Kind of school.
   (3) Location.
   (4) Course of study.
   (5) List of teachers and officers of the school.
   (6) List of students.
   (7) Funds and methods of maintaining.
   (8) List of text books and reference books.
   (9) Teaching and athletic equipment and specimens.

4. When the educational administrative office finds that a registered school is not well managed or has poor records, it may withdraw the registration.

5. If a registered school wishes to close or change it must petition the educational administrative office for permission.

6. After receiving permission to be established a school must apply for registration within three months.

7. If a school is not registered its students and graduation requirements cannot be recognized.

8. These regulations go into effect on the date of their proclamation.

TEN ITEMS OF TEMPORARY PRACTICAL APPLICATION FOR PARTYNIZED EDUCATION BY THE BUREAU OF EDUCATION OF THE COMMISSION OF POLITICAL AFFAIRS OF FUKIEN.

1. Every school shall hold a weekly memorial service to Dr. Sun Yat Sen on Monday. (Order of Service and Regulations enclosed herewith in separate copies.)

2. Every school shall have one hour's course on the Three People's Principles each week. The teacher of this course is to be engaged by the school, and confirmed by the Bureau (of Education).

3. Text books in each school shall be examined on the principle that they shall not be inconsistent with the Party principles.

4. Every school must post the news about the progress of the Revolutionary army: slogans, publicity works, and pictorial papers.

5. Every school must provide various literature on Partynized Education for reference readings for its teachers and students. There shall also be organized a book store for the purpose of introducing publications relating to the Party.

6. Every school must from time to time engage scholars who are versed in the Three People's Principles to give public lectures on the Party principles; the people of the locality shall be welcome to attend. There shall also be provisions to promote interest in attendance but they shall not be inconsistent with the idea of propagating the Party ideals.

7. The Boy Scouts of every school shall be uniformly changed into the Party Boy Scouts. (The Oath and Regulations of the Party Boy Scouts are enclosed herewith in separate copies.)

8. Each school shall utilize every celebration gathering to effect Party Propaganda according to the publicity principles of the Party.

9. There shall be regular investigations into any anti-party principle propaganda by the teachers and officers of every school. When it is discovered there shall be immediate prohibition, or punishment and dismissal.

10. There shall be sent forth special persons who are well versed in the partynized education to every school and church school to carefully observe whether or not they are conducted strictly according to the principles.

REGULATIONS OF THE WEEKLY MEMORIAL SERVICE

Art. 1. This Society for the purpose of permanently remembering our Last Chief; and for making all of our comrades affected by his spirit of strife and sacrifice for all the people; inspired by his personality of wisdom, love and courage, and determined to continue on striving for carrying through his principles; especially decides to have all organizations of the People''s Party of China as well as the agencies under the People's Government and all military groups observe a weekly memorial service.

Art. 2. The Weekly Memorial Service shall take place on each Monday morning any time from 9 to 12. The period of service shall not be over one hour. The time may be changed according to special conditions.

Art. 3. The Chairman of the service shall be a regular committee man in the case of the various classes of the People's Party of China, and the highest officer in charge in case of the government agencies and military groups of the locality.

Art. 4. Order of Service:
    (1) Congregation standing.
    (2) Three bows before Last Chief's Picture.
    (3) Chairman reading Last Chief's Will, congregation following.
    (4) Three minutes' meditation with lowering heads before the Last Chief's Picture.
    (5) Speech or Report on Politics.
    (6) End of Service.

Art. 5. The Central Executive Committee will distribute hand bills in the form of the party certificate, each with a picture of Last Chief, his will, mottoes, and these regulations, for all to follow.

Art. 6. Should there be discovery of non-energetic execution of the Memorial Service or secret connivance in evading it by open pretensions, the responsible regular committee man or the officer in charge shall be besides being dismissed given other treatment.

Art. 7. All members of the People's Party of China who must attend the service in accordance with their professions or other relations, must gather together before the Memorial Service begins. They shall not be absent consecutively for three times; there will be punishment for such a violation.

Art. 8. These regulations go into effect on the day when they are passed by the Central Executive Committee.

Note: These regulations apply to all the organizations and military

THE SITUATION IN CHINA 43

groups, hence it is provided that the service be presided over by the highest officer of the locality. Now that these regulations are applied to the school, the principal of the school shall be the presiding officer.

DECORATION OF MEMORIAL SERVICE HALL

In the Service Hall:
  In the middle—Dr. Sun Yat Sen's Picture.
  Above the picture—National and Party Flags.
  On both sides of the Picture:
    "The Revolution is not yet a success."
    "Comrades must fight on."
  Below—Dr. Sun Yat Sen's Last Will.
  Platform.
  Pillars and walls of Hall decorated with the various slogans of the Party.

Exhibit C.

MAJOR ISSUES IN CHINA
AS SUGGESTED BY MISSIONARIES IN FOOCHOW

1. The place of the missionary in the China of tomorrow.
2. The registration of schools.
3. The development of an indigenous Chinese Church.
4. The church and its relation to community life.
5. The relation of the missionary to the new movements in China.
6. How can America be kept informed correctly on the situation in China?
7. What is to be the future policy of the Board of Foreign Missions toward China?
8. The holding of property in China.
9. The hospital situation in Foochow.
10. What are to be the relative emphases on different phases of Christian work in China?
11. List and define the factors or tendencies that are now actually affecting our Christian work.
12. The problem of self-support.
13. The education in America of Chinese workers for the Christian ministry in China.
14. Emergency budget due to the various evacuations.
15. The future ratio of missionaries to the operating budget.

Exhibit D.

SUGGESTED AGENDA
For Discussion in Shanghai, May 5, 1927

1. Devotions.
2. Statement of results desired.
3. The Missionaries.
    (1) Emergency financial needs due to evacuation.
    (2) How long should missionaries be kept waiting for settled conditions?
    (3) How far shall consular advice be considered in return of missionaries to stations?
    (4) What should be our advice to missionaries who have returned to America?
    (5) What factors should determine their return to China?
    (6) How long may the Board and the Society be expected to provide for them?

THE SITUATION IN CHINA

    (7) Should definite plans be made to reduce missionary personnel?
4. The Church.
    (1) Shall we continue undiminished support of the Chinese Church, irrespective of failure of self support?
    (2) Shall we make effort to eliminate ineffective workers?
    (3) Shall we encourage the movement toward an independent Church?
    (4) Should we encourage the election of Chinese bishops? On what basis?
5. Education.
    (1) What minimum of religious work shall we require, to justify opening of schools and use of missionary money?
    (2) Shall we allow a faculty, or any member, to be appointed by Nationalists? Shall we permit Nationalist control of subject matter in any given course? Shall we permit the appointment by the Nationalists of a "proctor"? Shall we permit student interference in choice of faculty or principal?
    (3) If schools are taken over by Nationalists and all religious work eliminated, should missionaries return if invited?
    (4) Should registration be postponed in hope of more liberal terms?
    (5) Should we have a Board or Boards of Trustees in America for Middle Schools to hold endowment funds?
    (6) Should we, if unable to carry on Christian educational work in China, attempt to establish schools outside for students who wish such schools?
    (7) Shall we continue grants to students? If so, on what basis?
6. Property.
    (1) Shall we transfer church property as soon as possible to the Chinese Church? How?
    (2) Should school and hospital property be transferred with church property?
    (3) Shall we accept reparations for destroyed property?
    (4) Shall we finish buildings in process of building?
    (5) Under what conditions shall we begin to build those buildings for which money is provided?
7. Finance.
    (1) On what basis should the estimates for 1928 be made?
    (2) How will the present conditions affect designated gifts? And how will this affect our appropriations for 1928?
    (3) Should there be a central publicity agency for this country, or should each mission carry on its own publicity measures in America? Relation of publicity to designated gifts.

Exhibit E.

SUGGESTED AGENDA FOR FUKIEN AREA GROUP MEETING

Shanghai, May 4, 1927.

1. General statement. Bishop Wallace E. Brown.
2. Impressions from Foochow and objects that we would like to attain in this meeting. Dr. Ralph E. Diffendorfer.
3. Reports from the Fukien Conferences.
4. Discussion:

Missionary personnel.
    (1) Should all missionaries, now absent from their posts, go back upon consular permission, or should the Chinese be asked to exercise their judgment in the matter?
    (2) What stability should be attained in Chinese affairs before missionaries are returned from the United States?

THE SITUATION IN CHINA 45

(3) How far should we go, at present, in seeking Chinese cooperation in our policy as to missionary personnel?
(4) If definite action has not already been taken in Foochow, what steps, if any, should be taken in reducing personnel?
(5) What will be the attitude of the Board in continuing salaries to missionaries who have accepted government appointment, and who continue work in property taken over by the Nationalist government?

Property.
(1) What policy is to be followed in the holding of property? Will the Board continue to hold its property or will steps be taken to hand it over to the Chinese?
(2) What is the attitude toward building projects?
    (a) Now under way?
    (b) For which funds are on hand?
    (c) Contemplated for the future?

Finance.
(1) On what basis should the estimates for 1928 be made?
(2) How will the present conditions affect designated gifts? And how will this affect our appropriations for 1928?
(3) Should there be a central publicity agency for this country, or should each mission carry on its own publicity work in the United States? Relation of publicity to designated gifts.

Changing conditions and future policies.
(1) Registration and our educational policy.
(2) Changing stress in missionary work caused by national control of educational and medical work.
(3) What qualifications should be sought among prospective missionaries? Any that are different from the past? Any different balance of qualities?
(4) What is the next step in further transfer of authority and responsibility to the Chinese?
(5) Should we, as missionaries, be actively for, passive to, or actively against Methodist participation in the proposed Chinese National Christian Church?

Exhibit F.

FINDINGS OF A GROUP OF BISHOPS AND MISSIONARIES OF THE METHODIST EPISCOPAL CHURCH, FIFTY-FOUR IN NUMBER, WITH DR. AND MRS. DIFFENDORFER.
Shanghai, May, 5, 6, 10, 1927.

A DEMOCRATIC WORLD CHURCH

The Methodist Episcopal Church, unique among all Protestant churches, holds in one organic fellowship the peoples of many races and nations. In its General and Central Conferences these races and nations sit in fellowship as children of one Father. This world-wide character of our Church, because of its connectional form of organization, offers an opportunity for the further development of this fellowship, and provides the means for discussion and development of a common mind and a common purpose among all the peoples of the world. It is our conviction therefore that the Methodist Episcopal Church has a distinct contribution to make towards the Christianization of international contacts.

MISSIONARY AIM

We wish to call attention to this statement of the missionary aim:
"The supreme and controlling aim of foreign missions is to make the

Lord Jesus Christ known to all men as their Divine Saviour, to persuade them to become His disciples, to gather these disciples into Christian Churches which shall be self-propagating, self-supporting and self-governing, and to cooperate as long as necessary with these Churches in the evangelizing of their countrymen, and in bringing to bear on all human life the spirit and principles of Christ."

In accordance with the above declaration as to the character of the Church to which we belong and the missionary aim, we join in the following statement relative to a variety of subjects that have to do with the problems immediately confronting our Chinese brethren, the Church in America, and ourselves.

INDIGENOUS CONTROL

The Discipline of our Church gives evidence that the General Conference early recognized the right of the growing Church in every land to indigenous control. Increasing provision has been made for the exercising of this right, through the organization of Central Conferences with gradually augmented powers.

We believe that in China the time has come when the Central Conference should be given such additional powers as will give it full administrative control. To this end we would recommend the following proposals.

1. *Bishops and the Central Conference.*

We favor the revision of the Discipline in such a way that the Central Conference may elect its own Bishops, have power to fix their salary and determine their number and place of residence. We ask the Executive Board of the Central Conference of Eastern Asia, at an early date, to study the question and to prepare a concrete detailed plan to be presented to the Church through Annual, Central, and General Conference.

2. *Special Session of Central Conference for Election of Chinese Bishops.*

As soon as possible after legislation has been approved by the General Conference authorizing election of Bishops by the Central Conference, we believe that a special session of the Central Conference should be called for such election.

3. *Transfer of Church Property to the Chinese Church.*

We believe that local church property in China should be transferred to a Chinese organization as soon as the same may be arranged. To this end we advise the incorporation of the China Section of the Executive Board of the Central Conference of Eastern Asia, and the transfer to it as soon as this is accomplished, of all title to local church properties by the Board of Foreign Missions. The Executive Board should arrange for such petitions to the Central Conference, the General Conference and the Board of Foreign Missions as may be needed for changes in Disciplinary provision and for the transfer of local church property.

RIGHT OF SELF DETERMINATION

We recognize that, ultimately, the Chinese will decide for themselves as to whether or not they will find the best expression of their Christian experience in organized church life by associating themselves with this world organization, but we hope that every opportunity may be given for the fullest discussion and comprehension on the part of the Chinese of what is involved in this relationship before action is taken.

SELF-SUPPORT

Chinese church leaders recognize the importance of self-support, and we are confident they will, of their own accord, increase the proportion of self-support as rapidly as possible until entire self-dependence is reached. We suggest that stress be laid upon voluntary service, intensive evangelism,

THE SITUATION IN CHINA   47

sacrificial giving, and the whole message of Christian stewardship. A program of gradual reduction of foreign subsidy to churches already organized should be planned, the Board of Foreign Missions and the Finance Committees cooperating therein, so that in individual churches there may be as rapid advance to full self-support as possible. Thus, increasingly, funds of the Board may be made available for further extension of Christian activity to the hundreds of thousands of cities, towns and villages which have no church organization and where the Gospel is seldom if ever preached. With these methods our faith sees a self-reliant, self-supporting Church as an accomplishment of the near future, and sees a constant increase in missionary spirit and activity.

CONTINUED SUPPORT FROM ABROAD

An entirely new set of conditions, stressful in the extreme, confront the Chinese Church today. In addition to the multitudes of unevangelized and the needs of our educational institutions, there are, especially, the distress and losses incident to famine, banditry and civil war; the lack of employment, the burdensome taxation and military levies facing our Chinese Christians. These make it impossible for them to meet these emergent demands and carry their own current expenses. It is therefore imperative that the cooperation of the American Church should be continued in full measure.

UNIFIED WORLD ORGANIZATION

In order to relieve the General Conference of administrative matters that relate only to the American section of the Church, we believe the time has come for the organization of a Central Conference in the United States to deal with the great mass of material which concerns only the Church in the United States, and which now consumes such a large proportion of the General Conference session. In this way, the General Conference would be free to deal manfully with those phases of organized church life that have to do with the visible expression of a world-wide sweep of love, fellowship and cooperation in building the Kingdom of God on earth.

EDUCATION—SUPPORT OF MIDDLE SCHOOLS

As to the importance of the middle schools, and as to the necessity of Mission support for these schools, we would call attention to the following paragraphs from the Report of the China Educational Commission:

"The Christian middle schools are at this stage the most vital part of the whole Christian enterprise. They influence young people at the time when they are making life decisions, choosing vocations, fixing personal habits and social attitudes, beginning to form permanent attachments to friends, masters, school, and church, and accepting or rejecting Christianity. They touch the great middle classes of society among which the Church is now growing and gaining its greatest strength. They do not produce the foremost leaders, but furnish the body of sturdy supporters of Christian society.

" . . . . It is not, however, likely that the Church itself can soon undertake the main support of this grade of school. Therefore the Missions should consider the support of their middle schools one of the first and largest items on their budgets. In some Missions this may mean closing primary schools or withdrawing from college work or definitely uniting with other Missions to make the middle school work strong."

In the matter of self-support, we believe that educational institutions should be considered apart from the organized church. Generally speaking, our middle schools have made great advances during the last few years in the matter of increased fees, as in other things, so that students in our schools are now generally paying for their education fully as much as students in church schools in America, when the cost of living is taken into account.

War, revolutions and famine have, for the time being, reduced enrollment in some centers so that, under these conditions, increased income from abroad is necessary if our middle schools are not to be discontinued in the same way as have most of our day schools.

Even in America, educational institutions are not expected to support themselves from student fees or local contributions, but are dependent upon large endowment funds. No argument need to be made in stating that similar conditions prevail in China and in larger measure. The resources of the Chinese Church are overstrained in bringing the evangelistic work to self-support. The middle schools can expect little or nothing for endowment from Chinese sources. The middle schools must continue to look to America for funds for upkeep and endowment.

A Board of Trustees in America

In some instances boards of trustees in America have been organized for middle schools, but it is obvious that, were all of our middle schools to thus organize, there would be an undesirable multiplicity of such boards. It is our judgment, therefore, that there should be organized in America one board of trustees for our middle schools in China, the primary object of which would be the holding in trust and the proper administration of endowment funds for our middle schools individually and collectively, entirely apart from the Board of Foreign Missions; and holding in these matters the same relationship as do the boards of trustees of the union universities. It is our judgment that this board should be constituted in America, because of the unsettled state of affairs in China and the general insecurity of investments here, and also because the Chinese Church has not yet available sufficient personnel experience in the handling of large financial matters.

Should it not be found practical to develop this plan in the very near future, some other means must be found for increased support for these schools, or the early closing of some of our best schools will be forced upon us.

Christian Schools and the Government

We recognize the right of a government to control its educational institutions. In establishing educational institutions in China, it has been our purpose to give opportunities for expression of patriotic aims and of national consciousness. We have sought to make the education we offer both Christian and patriotically Chinese. We have emphasized above the importance of education in the life of the Church. In scientific educational work, the student desires and should be given the opportunity for thoroughgoing, unbiased investigation of all those forces and factors entering into and holding civilization. On the basis of Christlike character, alone, can there be good will among men that will make a true democracy possible; on that basis alone, can there be that mutual sympathy among nations and races whereby peace on earth may become a reality. The building of this character is the greatest contribution that the Church can make to China and to the world. We earnestly hope that in all regulations put forth by the government, there may be no limitations placed upon the full development and use of these essential elements of culture.

Minimum Requirements

We again state our willingness to meet the requirements of the government so long as religious liberty is recognized. Therefore, we recommend as the minimum of religious work offered in schools of middle school or college grade, justifying Mission support:
1. Elective courses in religious education shall be offered.
2. Voluntary attendance at religious services shall be permitted.

The School Staff

The efficiency of our schools in producing character is determined by the degree in which character is possessed by the staff of the school. In

THE SITUATION IN CHINA 49

making up and recruiting a school staff, the responsible authorities of the school should select from candidates of adequate scholastic attainments those whose lives and characters give the best evidence of being able to inspire and aid students to the attainment of Christlike life.

GOVERNMENT REGISTRATION

We are in favor of registration of our schools with the government, as soon as it can be accomplished without seriously compromising their Christian character.

In view of the fact that the regulations concerning registration of Christian schools in various provinces and lesser districts under Nationalist control vary greatly, we recommend that our institutions delay registration with the government until the government has become more stable and uniform in its requirements. This recommendation is made only in view of the circumstances immediately confronting us.

ADVICE TO MISSIONARIES

1. It is our clear conviction that the right of the individual conscience to determine personal action on debatable issues should be carefully respected. We also recognize the moral obligation carefully to consider the ethical consequences of an act under varying circumstances, whether those consequences concern international relationships, the fundamental welfare of those whom we have come to serve, or that of our fellow missionaries. The decision having been made, it becomes us to manifest in Christian love our commendation of those who, having been guided by the same principles, have arrived at different conclusions as to their personal duty, and who are ready to make great sacrifices in accordance with their decision.

2. It is our judgment that as many as possibly can, should remain in or near China, and, by relating themselves to other work or to study, with the Board's or Society's support, be ready for possible early return.

3. That those who feel, from circumstances of their own determination, under the conviction that they should return to America, either temporarily or permanently, ought to be permitted to do so with our full approval, and the approval of the regularly constituted authorities.

4. With regard to the time and conditions of return to our stations or elsewhere in China, we are convinced that the following principles should obtain:
   (a) We should await such a change in conditions as shall make practically inoperative the factors which determined our withdrawal in the first instance.
   (b) We should expect much progress in self-dependence and self-determination, due to readjustments and constructive experimentation on the part of those Chinese co-laborers who have been compelled by circumstances to take over our work. When we return, there should be such adjustments in appointments and such sympathetic approach, as carefully to conserve every gain in Chinese leadership brought about by the stimulus of these emergent conditions.

In view of the present developments of the Church in China and of Chinese consciousness as regards the return of missionaries to their fields of labor, we rejoice that in the establishment of our Church in China, in which we have membership, full provision is made in our normal procedure for the expression of the desires of the Chinese.

Exhibit G

INTERVIEW WITH MR. STERLING FESSENDEN, CHAIRMAN, MUNICIPAL COUNCIL, SHANGHAI

(All will recognize the significance of a statement from a man in Mr. Fessenden's position. By agreement, stenographic notes were made of the interview, but it has been impossible for Mr. Fessenden to read these notes.)

"The reason why the British defense force is in Shanghai is not due entirely to Shanghai itself or to the great financial interests which the British have here, but because the British Government is convinced that Soviet Russia, acting through the illiterate classes of China, is trying to strike a terrible blow at Great Britain. Silas Strawn placed the illiteracy of China at ninety-seven per cent. Russia realizes that if she can drive the British out of China by agitation, it would be a terrible loss of prestige for all white races in Asia and a terrific reaction would come in India. Shanghai is the keystone position. The nationalist leaders made a desperate attempt to take Shanghai and are now bitter against the foreigners. For the mere protection of Shanghai, the British Government would not send troops.

"All classes of Chinese were determined to down Shanghai. In 1925, I sent a request to fifty managers of the leading commercial houses to tell them what we were facing. After the shooting on May 30, 1925, came a tremendous internal upheaval, with a strike of the water and light employees. We survived that. The southern army got here in March, 1927. There were two Chinese armies fighting on the borders of the city, both of them hostile and anti-foreign, incited by the radical element.

"I called together the consular representatives of America, Great Britain, Japan, France, and Italy. If it had not been for British troops at that time, Shanghai would have gone down in a welter of blood. On March 21 there were 1,500 marines in the harbor. With the aid of wire barricades, we determined to hold the city. The British troops were quartered inside the city.

"The only way to defend Shanghai was to make the military line outside the city itself. I arranged with the British that, on my call, they would man that boundary. The British troops manned the barricades. The American marines would not take their places because of orders from Washington: 'We will not permit the armed forces of the United States to oppose any regular troops of China, whether southern or northern.' If worst came to worst, American troops could be used to protect American lives."

"There were 10,000 British troops, 2,000 volunteers, 2,500 police, 1,500 American marines, together with Dutch, Spanish, and French marines. Even then we had to abandon one salient. North and south were fighting, two great armies. The moderate wing and the radical wing of the nationalists outside were determined to get to Shanghai, and inside was a great mob of workmen, laborers, and civilians sympathetic with the southern army. At that time there were, at least, 30,000 foreign troops, but they were holding the line against a great horde from two armies with a great mob of radical civilians. If the line had broken, there would have been terrible loss of foreign life."

Mr. Fessenden spoke frequently of the "legitimate aspirations of China." "The trouble," he continued, "is the appalling ignorance of China. Ideas have been put into their minds by the Russians. There is a latent hatred of the foreigner, which in normal times is suppressed. When unusual conditions arise, that is unleashed. That is the appalling danger."

When asked if that hatred was found among the educated Chinese and business men, Mr. Fessenden replied, "No, not at all. But that class which is the largest element in China has been played upon and aroused. These mobs are like wild beasts, foaming at the mouth. They are just as bad to their own people."

Continuing, he said, "We are all sympathetic, in principle, with the Chinese idea that under extraterritoriality China is not on a plane of equality with the other nations of the world. We can sympathize to a certain extent with their desire to put China on a plane of equality. But what we resist is their method. They want to accomplish by force overnight what would really take China years to accomplish. All this propaganda about China having no say in governing Shanghai is a misrepresentation. In the first place, the only reason that foreigners were given extraterritoriality is because the Chinese have no conception of law and justice as we understand it. They are back in the prehistoric days. All that the Chinese have got

THE SITUATION IN CHINA 51

to-day in the way of education, hospitals and sanitation has come from the foreigner and through their contact with the foreigner. The Chinese villages have not changed in 5,000 years. With the advent of the missionary and the business man these schools and institutions were established. Chinese students in America are made a fuss over. Even with Western education they are not received on a basis of equality. They want to do by sudden change what ought to be done by evolution. Here is a city which has brought hundreds of thousands employment, and which has given safety to many. They would kick us all out to-morrow if they could. Three members of the Shanghai municipal council (out of fifteen) could now be Chinese, but the Chinese want a majority.

"This city represents an enormous investment. It has a bonded indebtedness of thirty million dollars gold. We welcome Chinese representation on the Council, but they must accept our proposition. America only has two representatives, Japan has two. All we want is reasonable security. There is no one Chinese city in the whole country that is decently administered. The Chinese official from the highest to the lowest looks upon a government position as a thing from which he can acquire a private fortune, not only for himself but for all his relatives and friends. If the Chinese could administer Shanghai or China, extraterritoriality would pass. Japan had extraterritoriality until 1895, and then it was no longer needed."

As to the way out of the present situation and whether there is a chance for the moderate wing to win out, Mr. Fessenden stated that he once thought so. "Now," he continued, "they are so torn up internally, among themselves, that I cannot be sure but that the whole nationalist movement will fail and the northern group win out as far south as Shanghai. Within the next two or three weeks (stated in early May, 1927) the northern troops will be back again.

Exhibit H.

PROPHETS AND THE PURPOSE OF GOD

(Address by Dr. Henry T. Hodgkin, in Martyrs' Memorial Hall,

Shanghai, May 4, 1927.)

The prophet is one who builds upon ultimate principles. He speaks not because any organization has told him to do so, but because he cannot keep silent. His authority is not that of the great men of the past, but that of an inward voice, which he knows is the voice of God. He is both an interpreter and a maker of history. He aims to change the whole current and trend of men's lives. His supreme end is to create a supreme organism animated by one spirit, the spirit of God himself.

It is men and women of this type that China needs far more than she needs statesmen and politicians. What good can the leaders in political life do unless there are stirrings in the hearts of the people out of a prophetic message from the living God?

If China needs prophets, what about ourselves? Six points in regard to the prophet and the purpose of God:

1. The prophet is one who is convinced that there is a divine purpose in human history. Sometimes the Church has not seen truly enough where God works. Because some of the results of modern science have the appearance of coming into conflict with some religious convictions, the Church has not clearly enough recognized the large elements of divine working in this great movement of science which is seeking to understand this creation. If we believe that Jesus Christ is the truth, we must believe that the passion for the truth is a divine gift to the world. The prophet is one who, seeing

the divine purpose, is thereby lifted above minor things, above the intrigues and jealousies of the world round about him. He lives in the sphere in which God works, and therefore has a message for the world.

2. The prophet is one who sees his own nation in its relation to the purpose of God. To interpret China's place in the world truly, we must see it in relation to the purpose of God. The prophet is the true friend of his nation. He is not one who says, "My country right or wrong." The nation has a place in God's purpose if it fulfills God's will, if it is honest in its public life, if it will put aside mobocracy and deceit.

3. The prophet sees that all nations are included in the purpose of God. Some of the finest fruits or flowers in the prophetic treatment are in Isaiah 19, when the prophet breaks forth on the universal note.

4. The prophet sees that the fulfillment of God's purpose involves suffering. This conception came to the great prophets through their own experiences and the experiences of the nations to which they belonged. It came to Jeremiah through long suffering and almost death. Isaiah 53 is a picture of suffering raised to its highest point. God's purpose was to come to mankind through vicarious suffering, and it required the death of Jesus Christ to make it live for the world.

5. The prophet is one who sees that God's purpose must prevail. He does not base his hope of the future upon endless calculation of possibilities. He has a certainty that does not fall down in the face of disappointment. His faith does not fail even though the immediate present may seem dark. Was not that spirit most of all exemplified when through the Garden of Gethsemane and the Cross itself there stepped the Redeemer of Mankind, who saw the glory that was to be revealed?

6. The prophet sees himself as having a part in working out the purpose of God. He has found that he has a relation to God, and it humbles him. Still through that moment of humility there is born the conviction which nothing can shake that he has a particular place of his own which it is up to him to fulfill in God's universe. It means that he is prepared to nerve himself for every effort to stand when every friend forsakes him, prepared to meet all the shafts which may be hurled at him, prepared to meet the shock when hopes fall, prepared to make his prayer life strong and active because God has put his finger upon him. With great humility, but with great courage and faith, he moves forward to obey. Paul: "Therefore, King Agrippa, I was not disobedient to the heavenly vision."

What about it when we think of our own particular problem in China today?

Isaiah 49: The picture of a prophet's experience. He is one who feels that God has chosen him. "I have labored in vain and have spent my strength in naught but that . . . . surely my judgment is of the Lord, I am recompensed of my God." The divine answer: "I will also give thee as a light to the Gentiles that thou mayest be my salvation unto the ends of the earth." He finds that God trusts him and calls him to a larger work than he ever dreamed of, to a task larger than he had ever dreamed of, at the very moment when he was on the point of lying down. There comes to him the challenge to rise and do something greater.

We are being summoned through this hour of difficulty to be men and women whom God can use for his larger service. In the light of this fact, let us turn back to see the six points as they concern ourselves.

1. There is a purpose of God in human history for our Chinese prophets as well as for ourselves. Let us get a new conviction of God as moving in the midst of his church, and transmit that conviction to those who are feeling the terrible stress and the temptation which comes to let down. Let us get a new hold today on a sense of God's purpose, and if our lives shall radiate that sense there is not anything we may not be able to do.

2. There is a special place for China among the nations. Many are not looking wistfully back into the past, but they are looking forward with hope,

some at least with idealism which is pure and sincere and splendid, some with a power of endurance and hope that means something for the future. Is it not for us to believe in the China that is to be! If there are darker days to come, fresh disillusionments, still we shall be there believing that the best is truest.

3. Let us remember that all nations are included in God's purpose. Over against hatred, let us lift up the universal love of God. Can we each of us in ourselves be the meeting point of at least two nations? Can we remind ourselves of the phrase in Ephesians: "He is the Christ of Peace who has broken down the middle wall of partition"?

4. The purpose must be reached through suffering. Is there danger that we think sometimes just a little too much of our own suffering and what we have lost? What have we bought with the cost? Let us hope we have not bought disillusionment, resentment, or despair. Let us hope we bought in the hour of suffering what the prophets bought while they were exiles in a foreign land. Let us get something that will give us fresh power to enter into the love of our Lord.

5. What are the prevailing forces in China today? Are they the forces of violence and ill will? Are they the forces which seem almost irresponsible as they sweep into the life of the nation? Are they only to be met by similar forces? It may be, for some of us at any rate, to show in our own personalities something of that kind of life which God expects of us. Perhaps it is a bigger thing than we ever thought of when God called us first to come to China. Perhaps there is something deeper than we thought we should ever have to pay.

6. I suppose every one of us can get back to some period in his life when he was so conscious of God's call to come out to China that he was conscious of a power lifting him up. Perhaps today the same great guide of our life is calling us to some great place in his purpose. Perhaps we are called not so much to administer and to lead, but to listen with the deeper understanding, quietly, patiently, to serve, to enter into the bitterness of other people's experiences, to take the lessons which come to us in such a spirit that the spirit of the Lord Christ is illuminated in us, to keep our faith bright through the darkest hours. Are these some of the calls which come to us? Is it perhaps now that in the time of enforced absence from loved work and workers we are being summoned by a fresh call? Let us use this time in quiet, humble thought. Let God's purpose be felt in every fiber of our being as we have never felt it. We are not blind to the facts—a thousand facts that would disappoint us and crush us—but the supreme fact is God. If we are so conscious of God that we have something of the prophetic fire burning in us, we will not run away from the facts. Look beyond the present; dream dreams. That is what it means to be a missionary these days.

Isaiah 60: Arise and shine, for thy light has come.

Exhibit I

SOME PROBLEMS CONFRONTING THE CHRISTIAN MOVEMENT IN CHINA AS SEEN BY A CHINESE CHRISTIAN

(An address delivered to a group of missionaries in Martyrs' Memorial Hall by C. Y. Cheng, D.D., Secretary National Christian Council, Shanghai.)

PRELIMINARY CONSIDERATIONS

I feel highly honored by being asked to address this important audience on the subject of "Some Problems Confronting the Christian Movement in China as Seen by a Chinese Christian." I propose to give a Chinese view of each of the following questions: Have the Chinese people pinned too much faith on the nationalist movement? Has the anti-Christian movement been too favorably considered by Chinese Christians? Is religious liberty being violated? Is the registration of Christian schools right and beneficial? Is the enforcement of party education in schools acceptable? How do Chinese Christians interpret the recent evacuation of missionaries from their posts? How is the Nanking incident regarded by Chinese Christians? Has the missionary enterprise succeeded or is it likely to succeed? What change, if any, is necessary in the work of Missions in China? Should Christianity speak on political matters? Has organized Christianity been unduly criticized by Chinese Christians? Is religious controversy unprofitable and harmful? Who are our worst enemies? Is there sufficient indication of a bright future for the Christian movement in China?

You will notice that these are all large questions, an adequate dealing of which requires separate treatment. I have, however, put them together in order that we may get a bird's-eye view of the situation as a whole. Under the limited time at our disposal, it is necessary to give in a very brief way an interpretation of these problems from a Chinese point of view. Further, I think we are still too close to these events that have been and are taking place to be able to see them in their true perspective. I have come with an open mind, willing to be convinced of a different interpretation and to seek for further truth. I shall be more than happy, if you will kindly allow me to benefit by your wisdom and experience in these matters.

One other word I wish to say before I start, namely, I am here representing no organization of any kind nor do I claim to speak for the entire Chinese Church. I am here only as a Chinese Christian, comparing notes with his fellow Christians of the West. I heartily invite your frank and candid criticism of my views regarding these matters, if such criticism is given in the spirit of Christian love. With your permission I now proceed to consider with you the questions proposed.

HAVE THE CHINESE PEOPLE PINNED TOO MUCH FAITH ON THE NATIONALIST MOVEMENT?

At least two kinds of views are being held by people in regard to this movement, namely, the extreme and the moderate. There are those who put all their faith in the movement and those who do not believe in it at all. Upon such extreme views we need make no comment just now. There are, however, many who see both the good and the bad in the movement, recognizing its possibilities as well as its dangers. Now the question is, which side weighs more heavily in our valuation of the movement, the brighter or the darker, since both are present? It is quite certain that most of the more thoughtful and intelligent people in China are watching this movement with the greatest interest, sympathy, expectation and hopefulness. China has suffered so much in these years, the heart of the people is reaching its breaking point in longing for a modern Moses to deliver the nation out of the oppression of Egypt to the land of promise. With the coming of the nationalist movement, people are watching it with all eagerness and enthusiasm, believing that through it, the salvation of the nation is to be realized. For this movement is not a mere political one—it touches upon the entire life of the nation, political, economic, social, moral, and religious. It is not only arousing the consciousness of the few in high places, but it is penetrating to people in all walks of life; even the less educated masses have felt the thrill of this great movement. We believe such aspirations are legitimate and necessary if China is to advance and grow at all.

But at the same time we cannot minimize, much less ignore, the ghastly side of the destructive and dangerous element in this otherwise wholesome and promising movement of the Chinese people. Bolshevik influence has already done a great deal of harm to China; it will do even greater harm if unchecked. The Chinese people are more than glad to find that both the Southern and Northern governments are taking definite measures against this sinister monster that seeks to pull down and to destroy. The innocent people who are in its iron grip in Central China are longing and praying for deliver-

THE SITUATION IN CHINA

ance from their agonizing suffering. The whole thing is contrary to the traditions and temperament of the Chinese people. While all this is true, the whole movement should not be condemned because of its undesirable elements. That would be suicidal.

The situation is capable of being interpreted and viewed from the more gloomy side, for even the less radical part of the movement is far from perfection. Defects and shortcomings are traceable in more places than one. But we maintain that with all its imperfections, it has furnished us sufficient inspiration and incentive to justify our high hopes that through the instrumentality of the People's Movement the future development of the Chinese nation will be furthered.

HAS THE ANTI-CHRISTIAN MOVEMENT BEEN TOO FAVORABLY CONSIDERED BY CHINESE CHRISTIANS?

As we all know, anti-Christian propaganda is not an organization but a movement. Because of this fact it is spreading very widely in the country and is very difficult to get hold of. Every one is at liberty to express his opinion and offer his criticism in whatever way he pleases. This makes it hard to secure a definite and clear view of the platform upon which they stand. All sorts of criticisms, attacks, charges, accusations, have been made against the Christian religion. Some are the result of prejudice, some of misunderstanding; some are worth careful consideration, while others are of no value at all.

Besides those accusations that can be nailed as the result of prejudice and misunderstanding, however, there is much in what these people say that is true. Since we believe in truth we cannot and must not ignore, at least, this part of the contribution of the anti-Christian movement. It must not be regarded as a sign of disloyalty to the Christian faith when we are ready to listen and accept this part of the criticism of the opposing forces.

We further believe that there are not a few who criticize the Christian religion who are in real earnest in seeking after truth and light, and to such we are ready to extend the right hand of fellowship, for we too are seeking further light and truth which we believe are best revealed in the person of Jesus Christ.

However, we are not ready to regard this movement as a friend of the Christian religion in a sweeping way. Toward those who have for their purpose the destruction of Christianity and the nullification of its work we shall forever stand in direct and uncompromising opposition. To meet prejudice with patience and forbearance? Yes. To meet misunderstanding with explanation and correction? Yes. To meet truth with ready sympathy and acceptance? Yes. But to identify the Christian movement with men who are unsympathetic and hostile to it? Never!

IS RELIGIOUS LIBERTY BEING VIOLATED?

Since the agreements reached between the Chinese government and Western nations, by which the former should protect those who propagate or follow the Christian religion in China, Chinese Christians have enjoyed religious toleration by virtue of such treaties. Not until the formation of the new republic, in 1911, was religious freedom granted in both the national and provincial constitutions. Technically speaking, Chinese Christians are now doubly protected by both Chinese constitutions and foreign treaties. In the national and provincial constitutions and those of the Kuomintang Party, religious liberty is clearly stated and recognized.

We think the granting of such religious freedom in the constitution is needed and important, not only because Christian people require such protection, but also because it is the duty of the government to look after the rights of the people and safeguard their interests. This is specially needed, because there is a growing feeling among Chinese Christians that they should not be protected by the Toleration Clauses in the so-called "Unequal Treaties," as these treaties were made under unhappy circumstances.

At present, Christianity is meeting with a great deal of opposition by the various forces that have no use for religion in general, or Christianity in particular. Much of this criticism and argument, these charges and accusations, can hardly be regarded as a violation of religious liberty. If Christians have the freedom to believe, others have also the freedom to disbelieve; if we are at liberty to embrace Christianity, others also are at liberty to adopt other religious faiths. But religious toleration is in danger of being violated when one religion is more favorably placed than other religions, as in the attempt made some years ago to establish Confucianism as the State Religion, or when specific religious practices and exercises are interfered with or forbidden, as is happening in many cases at the present time in provinces south of the Yangtze River. For religious liberty means at least two things—freedom and equality—freedom for people to adopt or propagate their own religion, so long as there is nothing in it contrary to the interests of the community, and equal treatment of all religious bodies by the government. If, as we Chinese Christians hope and believe, the true principles of the Republic prevail, we do not question the ultimate establishment of these rights. Nevertheless, we realize that the power of the authorities to carry out this provision is not now sufficient and, in the meantime, there is persecution and danger to the Christian Church.

As the country is still in the midst of a severe political struggle and military conflict, and as religious liberty is fully recognized in the constitutions of the national and provincial governments, we may reasonably expect that in a more settled condition this matter will be adequately dealt with and fully enforced. For the time being we have to suffer some inconveniences and discomforts which are by no means confined to Christian people. But we believe it is the duty of the Christian Church to make a study of the situation in this connection and to make an effort to see that this rightful liberty is safeguarded, not for themselves alone but in relation to all religions.

With regard to the freedom of missionaries in China to propagate the Christian faith in the future, we hope they will seek to dissociate themselves from the worn out treaties, and to support the making of new ones based on the principles of reciprocity, equality, and good will to the satisfaction and benefit of both parties. In truth, there is little in the so-called Toleration Clauses that can be regarded as objectionable; what makes them the target of criticism is their association with out-of-date treaties. They are a good thing in a bad place.

Is the Registration of Christian Schools Right and Beneficial?

As citizens of China we think we should comply with the requirement of the government with regard to the registration of our schools. We would even go further and say that not only our schools should be registered in the government but also our churches and other Christian institutions as well. And this for two reasons: first, Chinese Christians must be loyal to their government and submit to its ruling; secondly, the Christian movement must be recognized by the government as a lawful and legitimate organization and entitled to its protection. The Chinese Christian Church of Peking, with which your present speaker was connected, was duly registered in the Ministry of the Interior as far back as 1912, the second year of the republic. A very kind reply was received from the ministry advising us "to follow the footsteps of the first two Chinese Christians, Tsai and Liang by name, baptized by Doctor Morrison over a century ago, to lead the Chinese people to come to the Saviour." Very good advice, given by the president of the Ministry of the Interior!

However, our present problems are more with the restrictions that have been attached to the registration than with the registration itself. Both the southern and the northern governments have attached many strings to the registration of Christian schools and such registration is required. With most of the restrictions we have little or no quarrel. In regard to the matter of religious instruction in our schools we have not yet reached a general agreement. Some feel that if religious instruction is not permitted in our schools, the real purpose of Christian education is practically lost; others feel, however, that educational work should be done for the sake of education and not to proselytize. It is more by Christian influence, they hold, than by religious exercises, that students are to be attracted to Christ. Such limitations, therefore, in no serious way curtail the usefulness of the educational work of the Christian Church. We readily agree that both views are well taken. Setting before the students a Christ-like life is, of course, a much harder task to perform than giving religious instruction and performing religious exercises.

In our judgment, if Christian schools are permitted to give religious teaching freely and to conduct religious worship—well and good. Few Christian educators would suggest the removal of them. But, since voluntary religious teaching and worship alone are permitted by the government under whose direction our work is to be carried on, there are the two courses open to us—to close our schools or to work under this limitation and make the best of it. We think the latter is the wiser course. This will put our work to a more severe test, but if it come out well, it will have an even greater and more lasting result. Under such circumstances, the securing of a teaching staff which truly represents the spirit of Christ becomes a great and yet more urgent necessity. If such suggestions are acceptable to institutions under the Chinese Church, they can also be applied in a general way to the schools of the Missions.

IS THE ENFORCEMENT OF PARTY EDUCATION IN CHRISTIAN SCHOOLS ACCEPTABLE?

The Kuomintang is leaving no stone unturned in converting people to an allegiance to the "Three Principles" stated by its leader, Doctor Sun. From the point of view of the nationalists, we can readily see the desirability of spreading this message to the whole nation, and the advantage for the future success of the nationalist movement in enforcing in all schools what is termed party education. This is particularly needed at the present juncture when these party ideals are not yet fully understood and accepted by the entire people. We must say that the amount of devotion and enthusiasm shown by the party command both our admiration and sympathy.

We are, however, less sure whether the enforcement of party education in all schools is to remain as a permanent part of education. We are not so sure that the field of education should be exploited by a political party; we are not so sure that school children or young students are fitted to play the game of party politics; we are not so sure that one political party can permanently hold the entire field. We are not so sure that the teaching of these principles in the hands of non-Christians may not be made, in places, the ground for an attack upon the Church or the occasion for inculcating ideas which are contrary to Christ's. Should any rivals enter the field, complications in the educational world will be serious and difficult to solve.

How Do CHINESE CHRISTIANS INTERPRET THE RECENT EVACUATION OF MISSIONARIES FROM THEIR POSTS?

The recent unexpected evacuation of missionaries from the interior has a few parallel cases in other countries, though the circumstances under which the evacuation took place are different. At times, evacuation was made unavoidable because of severe religious persecution; or because of definite orders from the government under which the missionaries work. The present evacuation is made by order of these governments, based upon a certain interpretation of the situation. This assumes that conditions may arise to justify such a course and after the Nanking incident much weight is given to this view.

The evacuation is capable of different interpretations in the minds of the average Chinese Christians. With their inadequate understanding of the significance of the sudden turn of affairs and of the necessity of this unexpected exodus, many are staggered and perplexed to know what to think or say. Not a few are influenced, less by this uniform evacuation by order of government than by stories of missionaries remaining in the work even to the point of sacrifice. Moreover, this evacuation of missionaries has resulted in Chinese Christians at short notice taking on much responsibility, in some cases, unfamiliar responsibilities. We shall hear later reports of both successes and failures, of encouraging and disappointing results. Again, we shall soon face the problem of the return of missionaries to their former place of trust. It is not too soon for Mission administrators and authorities to begin to consider this problem.

We are very sorry that our missionary friends have been placed in such a situation; we understand that many have not accepted this sudden change with any satisfaction and, indeed, it has greatly disturbed their plans and programs. It humbles us to think that China is considered a land not safe for our foreign friends to live in, and that prompt departure from the country should seem to be a necessity.

Now, how are we to interpret this spectacle? Do we see any purpose in this turn of events? A lady missionary believes that there is a twofold purpose of God in this unexpected change: first, to deliver the Chinese Christians from depending too much upon the help of their missionary friends and to develop native talent and initiative; secondly, to save the missionary worker from putting too much trust in his organizing, administrative and directing ability and to have more confidence in his Chinese fellow workers. If recent events will fulfill this twofold purpose, we have ample reason to give thanks to the Almighty for this great blessing in disguise.

How Is the Nanking Incident Regarded by Chinese Christians?

All right thinking Chinese regret most deeply the unhappy affair which happened in Nanking and nearby cities, where missionaries, together with some Chinese Christians and other foreigners, were so badly treated by the revolutionary troops and local bad characters. We are ashamed that such a thing has happened to our missionary friends who were so full of sympathy with the aspirations of the Chinese people. This incident was a blow not only to our foreign friends, but also to the Chinese people, excepting, of course, those, probably from up river, who staged this sinister movement largely for political purposes.

We wish to express our deep sense of admiration for the Christ-like spirit manifested by the friends of Nanking. We wish further to say that we are quite at one with them in making a truthful statement about what they had experienced in that dark day, even though such statement might be to China's hurt. We say this because it is our conviction that, if China is to rise and advance at all, her national aspirations must have truth as their foundation; otherwise no amount of revolution can effect real transformation.

We wish also to be permitted to state that, during the present political struggle and military operations, it is an open secret that the men who are seeking to shape the destiny of the nation have their hands more than full in keeping good discipline in the fighting forces; in directing the activities of the People's Party; in adjustments between the old order and the new; above all, in experimenting and testing the new government. These and many other things constitute a task by no means easy, especially when the opposing forces are still uncurbed. This is not to justify the ugly things done in Nanking, not in the least. It rather shows what an extra amount of the Christian virtue of patience is required in considering the affairs of to-day if we are really interested in, and have sympathy with, the national aspirations of the Chinese people.

Has the Missionary Enterprise Succeeded or Is It Likely to Succeed?

We make no apology when we say that neither is organized Christianity perfect nor are all missionaries saints. It does not take much trouble to prove this to be true. There is still much in the Christian Church that is unsuitable, uncongenial, unacceptable and out-of-date. There are still many men and women who do not reveal the attractiveness and beauty of Jesus Christ and who are more a hindrance than a help to the Christian cause. Indeed there is much room for improvement in both the work and the workers.

But, at the same time, we cannot be blind to the manifold blessings that have come to us through the lives and work of the missionaries in China. In the lives of not a few we do see the reproduction of the Master. Many Chinese Christians will forever bless God for the lives of such missionary men and women.

Some of the outstanding missionary achievements are monumental witnesses in China which cannot possibly be gainsaid or denied: the introduction to the Chinese people of the world's Saviour and Friend; the enlightenment of the ignorant; the uplift of the oppressed; the healing of the sick; the education of the young; the improvement of social conditions; the cultivation of cultural intercourse; in a hundred and one ways China has been served and helped by the missionary body which is the best friend of the Chinese people. It is true that the missionary has not yet reached his ideal, for the ideal is high; but the measure of success attained is sufficient to indicate a future of great usefulness.

Allow me to go one step further: the success of the Christian religion will be doubled or tripled when certain defects and shortcomings are removed. Indeed there is no reason to think that the bottom of Christianity is dropping out or that its days in China are numbered. Let us trace the rainbow through the rain; let us ride forth in faith till we enter upon a yet greater day!

WHAT CHANGE, IF ANY, IS NECESSARY IN THE WORK OF MISSIONS IN CHINA?

That China needs Jesus Christ and his message of love we are convinced. But the presentation of that message needs to be reconsidered from time to time in order to meet the requirements of the day. With the very rapid change of events in China, it is essential that such an evaluation should be made. If the Christian Church is to perform its task with freedom, certain obstacles must be removed. These obstacles are blocking the way to progress. There are certain problems now engaging the attention of Christian leaders, both Chinese and missionary, namely, such questions as church independence, church union, devolution of foreign missions, developing the indigenous church, co-operative activities, etc. Why independence? Because there is the obstacle of dependence. Why union? Because there is division. Why devolution? Because there is the need for it. Why an indigenous church? Because the church is still a foreign institution. When we have solved these problems, the Christian Church will have a better chance to go forward and accomplish its task of introducing men to God and God to men through Jesus Christ.

In order to remove these obstacles and enable the Christian Church to move more rapidly forward in performing its task, we would venture to suggest that foreign missions should, in future, consider the work more in terms of a Christian fellowship, sharing with the Chinese Church its successes and failures, joys and sorrows, ups and downs. Let us, in this great fellowship, work together for the solution of these urgent and vital problems that are confronting us, the removal of the foreign stigma upon the religion of Christ; the development of a Christian Church that is really of the people, for the people and by the people; the linking together of the various divisions in the Christian Church; the cultivation of the spiritual experiences of the Chinese Christians; the enlargement of the religious outlook of Christian people so that it penetrates all departments of life, personal, social, national and racial.

Let the relationship between Church and Mission never be based on dollars and cents; employer and employed; giving and receiving. Let it be a great Christian fellowship, sharing each other's experiences, problems, sufferings, hopes. We believe such a change of attitude will, in some measure at least, help forward the progress of the Christian movement in China.

THE SITUATION IN CHINA

SHOULD CHRISTIANITY HAVE ANY VOICE IN MATTERS POLITICAL?

Probably there is general agreement among Christian people, that the individual Christian cannot and should not be indifferent to the political development of his country. As a citizen of a nation, he has a duty to perform in helping forward the work of the nation and to see that the government is performing its task faithfully and honestly. Such a duty is in no sense contrary to his being a follower of Jesus Christ. But as to the Christian Church, it is undesirable that it should identify itself with party politics, for the simple reason that the work of the Church is for everybody and must not be limited to any particular political organization or party. History has abundant proof that when the Church allied itself with the government, the result was none too happy. In fact a great deal of harm was done to both government and Church. We believe there is a general agreement on these two points, namely, that individual Christians may interest themselves in politics but, tnat the Christian Church must refrain from doing so.

In our midst there are people who feel that under no circumstances should a Christian Church or organization express itself in regard to political affairs. Others, however, feel that, under certain conditions, Christian bodies should express themselves in regard to political matters, especially when a moral issue is involved and when the Christian Church is affected by the problem. Ordinarily, the Church takes no part in party politics, but when a moral issue and the work of the Christian Church are involved in such matters, her voice should be raised. No Christian is willing to admit that, while the principles of Christianity can be applied to the personal, family and social life, yet the political sphere is forbidden ground upon which Christianity cannot trespass. That would be saying that the principles of Jesus cannot be applied in this field. Many of the Old Testament prophets were men who voiced the will of God regarding the national destiny of the Hebrew people. They were essentially great figures in national affairs. In the present struggle for China's national existence, we do need such strong men, like the prophets of old, to put China's house in order, and we have no reason to think that Christian men cannot be such prophets. May not the Church, too, on occasion, lift up her prophetic voice and speak clearly on great public questions? To sum up, the Christian Church is neither a running dog of the political machine nor an institution that lives in water-tight compartments. It is not easy to draw the line. Discrimination and care must be exercised in dealing with such matters.

HAS ORGANIZED CHRISTIANITY BEEN UNDULY CRITICIZED BY CHINESE CHRISTIANS?

The so-called Renaissance movement of a few years ago has distinctly left its legacy to the young people of China, namely, the spirit of criticism. They put a question mark to almost everything in life, traditional, customary, ethical, moral, social, political, religious and what not. They take nothing for granted; every thing must be scrutinized and studied. This critical spirit has also found its way to the Christian Church. So not a few young and thoughtful Christians in China have been studying the practices, traditions, teachings, rituals, methods of the Christian Church with this critical spirit of the time.

This spirit of criticism has annoyed some and staggered others. People feel uncertain as to the direction in which they are going. They also feel that Christianity is being pulled to pieces not only by the hostile world outside, but also by some people within. This fear is not altogether imaginary, because we do find that various motives have lain behind this spirit of criticism. Indeed there are some who rather delight in finding out the failings of the Christian movement. They are happier to dwell upon the shortcomings of the Church than upon its achievements. These failings do not seem to hurt their sense of loyalty to Jesus Christ. They rather like to think of the Christian movement in terms of its darker side. With such people,

THE SITUATION IN CHINA

indeed, we have no sympathy. We are sorry that criticism has been used as a kind of weapon to deliver blows upon the Christian Church in which they claim fellowship.

Apart from this undesirable attitude shown by some, we rather think the exercise of this critical faculty in regard to matters religious has been more beneficial than harmful. Notwithstanding the many half-baked ideas that have been expressed, the immature judgments that have been stated, the blunders and mistakes that have been made, we are of opinion that this critical study of organized Christianity has helped many to a better understanding and greater appreciation of the work of the Christian Church. In not a few cases the Church has been helped by these criticisms. This spirit of criticism is, we believe, far better than the former attitude of indifference to the work of the Church, or the habit of swallowing everything that is given by others without proper mastication.

Is Religious Controversy Undesirable and Harmful?

Many people dislike the word "controversy," thinking it is something disagreeable, unfriendly and antagonistic. But we think otherwise. In practically nothing do we think alike. How can we expect that we should in matters of religion. It is an impossibility. Progress can only be achieved when we differ, and our differences open the way to greater light and deeper truth. Even in our own thinking there is frequent change. We are often inconsistent. That is not necessarily a bad thing. Often it shows that our mind is growing. We think controversy rather a helpful element than a hindering one. Religious controversy often means a real blessing to both parties, so that men are enabled to see not only one side but both sides of the shield.

But, if such a religious controversy is to be made really beneficial and helpful, there is one condition that must be strictly observed, otherwise it does more harm than good. The one condition that is absolutely essential is what we call "Christian sportsmanship," which is another way of saying the love-spirit of Jesus Christ. If we cannot keep up that love-spirit, we are treading on dangerous ground when we enter upon such controversy. We do not pray for the removal of religious disagreement, for we do not think it helps matters if we all think alike. But we do earnestly pray that the spirit which was in Christ Jesus may bring us to the state in which we can safely engage in such religious controversy. We are not qualified to enter upon this field of Christian activities, if we do not possess the virtue of Christian sportsmanship. By this love-spirit or the absence of it, we will be judged.

Who Are Our Worst Enemies?

That we have many enemies is a fact that calls for no argument. We think the anti-Christian movement that seeks for the destruction of Christianity is an enemy. The communistic teachings that have nothing to do with religion and are hostile particularly to Christianity are an enemy. The materialistic and atheistic views of life, which believe that there is no need of a God in this scientific age and would have nothing to do with the spreading of religion, may also be regarded as our enemies. The personal, social, national and racial sins of various kinds that are working directly in opposition to the work of the Christian religion are certainly the enemies of Christianity. All these can be found in China to-day. So the Christian Church is face to face with many strong opposing forces. It is like a spiritual tug of war and the decisive hour has not yet come.

But these are forces from without and are comparatively easy to deal with. We have enemies worse than all of these. At present there is a good deal of trouble in China. Many Christian people have suffered much, but we are unhappy to say, in quite a few cases the troubles they have met were caused, not so much by the outside forces, but by the dissatisfied and discontented people within the Christian Church. I need hardly illustrate this point. It is familiar to us all. Suffice it to say that the enemies within are worse than those without. Furthermore, we have our worst enemies often within ourselves—the spirit of narrow nationalism, of social distinctions, of unfairness, of inconsideration, of impatience, of despair, of unpreparedness, of uncharitableness, that have revealed themselves in word and deed, are surely the worst enemies we have to face. We can never hope to overcome the evil forces without, if we cannot clear ourselves of these forces of darkness within us.

ARE THERE SUFFICIENT INDICATIONS OF A BRIGHT FUTURE FOR THE CHRISTIAN MOVEMENT IN CHINA?

Yes, there are. Let us briefly mention a few of them. We must recognize, in the first place, that, while there has been such a political upheaval during the past few years, the essential character of the Chinese people remains practically the same. We see the great waves and billows that are surging on the surface of the sea, but there is still that essential calm underneath. It is reasonable to hope that, when the passing cloud has blown over, the bright sky will again appear on the horizon.

Again, in this national movement of the Chinese people, with all the undesirable things that have alarmed us, we see the signs of life and that life will surely grow. The sick man is beginning to recover from his illness. The sleeping lion is beginning to awake. These signs of life are seen, not so much in the political changes, but in the growing national consciousness of the people which clearly indicates a great future for the work of the Christian enterprise.

Surely the seed of the Christian Church planted in China years ago is breaking through the earth and sending up its sprouts. To be sure, there are still many signs of youth, but we are sure that since there is life there must be growth. For the nurturing of such a young Church, for the assisting of such a forward movement, for the establishing of such a Christian fellowship between the East and the West, in a hundred ways the Christian missionary can be of invaluable service. We might go on mentioning other indications, but we can feel sufficiently sure that we may look upon the future work of the Christian movement with assurance and encouragement.

Exhibit J.

SUGGESTED AGENDA

For Discussion, Peking, May 17-18, 1927.

I. PROPERTY

1. Shall property in China continue to be vested in the Board at New York, or shall we begin to turn it over to the Church in China?
(a) The question of deeds and titles, and the stamping of deeds.
2. What about the protection of property?
3. What is to be done about obligations on property?
4. What is meant by property transfer? To what forms of property does this apply? What is to be the disposition of properties held in China by the Board and the Society for revenue purposes?

II. MISSIONARY PERSONNEL

1. What provision shall be made for missionaries who are on forced leave of absence from their stations? How shall they be occupied until their return?
2. What provisions shall be made for the return of missionaries who may be specially needed, and under what conditions will they return?
3. What voice shall be given to the Chinese in the determining or influencing of the recall of missionaries to the field, who have gone to America on furlough or for other causes?

THE SITUATION IN CHINA 63

4. What is the place of the missionary in the future program of the Christian movement in China?
5. Has the time come for a radical reduction in the missionary staff? What are the factors?
6. Is the salary support of missionaries in China adequate?
7. What are the factors to be taken into account in the selection and training of new missionaries?
8. Shall the missionary budget be subject to redistribution on the field by either missionary or joint groups, or shall the Board be entirely responsible for the determination of that budget?
9. Shall the local Chinese group be given a voice in the determining of the appointments of missionaries on the field? If so, how?

III. MISSIONARY POLICY

1. What forms of missionary work at the present time should be emphasized?
2. What is the method by which our major missionary policies in China are to be studied and evaluated in the future? The time for such an evaluation, if it is found necessary?
3. What shall be the policy on the field with regard to cooperation between the Society and the Board?
4. What place do funds from America have, in the future, in the development of church and institutional life in China? What is to be the form of administration of finances from abroad?
5. To what extent, and how rapidly, shall there be a change in our administrative policy?
6. If it is desirable to transfer the administration of the Church in China to Chinese, what course shall be followed to bring that about?
7. In view of the present situation, ought we to consider complete withdrawal from certain fields of work in China? On what basis?
8. What is to be our future policy with regard to concentration of effort as over against expansion?
9. What is to be the place of religious education in our future program?
    a—Through the churches.
    b—Through Christian schools.
    c—Through government schools.

IV. THE CHURCH IN CHINA

1. Are we to pursue the policy of establishing the Methodist Episcopal Church in China as a part of our international organization, or are we to work for the development of an independent Church in China?
2. Has the time come for the election of Chinese to the episcopal office? What is the course to be followed?
3. Under our present organization, how far are the Chinese able to express themselves in the development of their own forms of religious expression and church organization?
4. What are the strengths and weaknesses of the Church in China, as we view them?
5. How can the development of responsible group action in the Church be secured?
6. Shall the present relationship between the Board and the Church in China be continued, or shall some such change be made as has come about, for example, in Japan?
7. What needs to be done for the securing and training of an adequate ministry for the Church?

V. EDUCATION

1. What is to be our policy with reference to the registration of Christian schools?
2. Are educationists in China free to experiment? Is there need for

experimental work in education? If so, in what directions? Has our education become standardized?
3. Is the religious life and atmosphere of our schools satisfactory? What is suggested?
4. What is to be the financial basis for our schools in the future?
5. What lines of educational work should we undertake?
   a—Normal education?
   b—Schools for nurses?

VI. GENERAL

1. What are the present tendencies in Chinese national life which are actually affecting the Christian movement?
2. What is to be the future of our medical work?
3. Shall we proceed with the present plans for holding a Central Conference for Eastern Asia at Seoul, Korea, in November, 1927? If not, what other plans shall be made? Shall China return to the organization of a Central Conference for China only?
4. What steps shall be taken to secure the adequate representation of educational and hospital work on the field finance committees?

Exhibit K.

WHAT IS INVOLVED IN JOINING THE KUOMINTANG PARTY?

(Information furnished by a group of senior students from Fukien Christian University at dinner in the home of President Gowdy.)

I. *A list of questions must be answered to determine what your belief is with reference to the party. These questions are as follows:*
1. What is your attitude toward Kuomintang?
2. What do you understand about the principles of Kuomintang?
3. What do you know about the present situation in China?
4. What do you know about the present world situation?
5. What work will you do for Kuomintang?

II. *A list of personal questions must also be answered, as follows:*
1. What is the economic condition of your family, i. e., are you able to devote your time to the service of the party?
2. Are there others dependent upon you for support?
3. What is your previous education?
4. What is your income?
5. How much do you spend?

This list of questions must be answered and sent in to the Central Committee. The application must be seconded by two members of the party. The applications must be written in duplicate. One is sent in with a photograph of the applicant, and the other is kept by the applicant. If the applicant is accepted, he is furnished with a certificate of membership in the party.

III. *Duties of members.*

1. The payment of monthly dues is required, on a graduated scale. Students pay two dimes (Mex.) a month. If a member fails to pay his dues for three months, his membership is revoked.
2. A member must be present at every meeting, unless he presents his excuse to the committee beforehand. If he is absent without letting the committee know, three times in succession, his membership is forfeited. The meetings are held locally.
3. Five members constitute a minimum for the organization of a local group. Five local groups constitute a district organization.
4. There are a representative committee, an executive committee, and a judicial committee in each group.

Exhibit L.

LETTER FROM ERNEST B. PRICE

AMERICAN CONSULAR SERVICE

Foochow, China, April 28, 1927.

Dr. Ralph E. Diffendorfer,
Secretary, Board of Foreign Missions of the Methodist Episcopal Church,
Foochow, China.

My Dear Dr. Diffendorfer:

With the thought that it might be useful to you to have in writing some of the observations I made in our verbal conversation of yesterday, I should like to summarize briefly certain of the ideas then expressed. Naturally, the present letter will touch only on matters affecting the Consulate officially.

THE EVACUATION OF AMERICAN CITIZENS

It is understood, of course, at the outset, that the points of view of an American Consul who advises Americans to leave his district and of the persons who accept the advice may not coincide. In short, the reasons why the Consul gives the advice may be quite different from the reasons why an individual American accepts it. I should like to give, briefly, first my own point of view, and second that of at least some of those who accepted my advice to leave.

One of the principal duties of an American Consul anywhere is the protection of Americans and their interests within his district. On the other hand, even in China, where the American Government enjoys the privilege of judicial jurisdiction over its nationals, the American Government looks primarily to the Chinese Government for the protection of Americans and their interests in China. Hence, so long as the Chinese Government, or a *de facto* local Government, displays the willingness and the ability to protect Americans and their interests, the American Government relies upon it to do so. Whenever the Chinese Government shows itself either unwilling or unable to extend protection, then the American Government must choose either to interpose its own protection or to advise Americans to leave. It has been sufficiently obvious, I think, that the American Government has chosen the latter course in China during the events of the past few months. Whether or not an individual citizen agrees with such a course is beside the point, so far as an American consular officer is concerned. A Consul does not make national policies; he follows them.

The events of January 14th to 17th of this year, with which you are familiar, convinced me as American Consul that the persons who, at the time, held the actual power in this region were not only unwilling to protect American life and property but were definitely committed to a policy of driving out at least a certain group of Americans and of seizing their properties. It was my duty to apprehend whether such a policy would endanger American lives, for only danger to life itself could justify me—in the absence of an announced policy of the American Government to withdraw all Americans from Nationalist-controlled territories—in advising Americans to leave this district. I would state here, frankly, that considerations of policy, for example whether the evacuation of a considerable group of Americans would help bring about a change in control or policy on the part of the local *de facto* authorities, held no place in forming my decision, which was based solely on the conviction that actual danger to American life existed. In my conversations with Americans gathered in conference at the Consulate I sought to make this point clear. It is as well to record here my conviction, however, that the evacuation of Americans did considerably help bring about a change in control and in policy of the local *de facto* authorities. It might be well further to record, at this point, that I am credibly informed that the man who unquestionably engineered the

Foochow affair of January 16th also engineered the Nanking affair of March 24th, which, as you know, was considerably worse. I am convinced that this man and his agents sought to bring about, in Foochow, precisely what they succeeded in bringing about in Nanking, and that their purpose was largely thwarted here by reason of the wholesale evacuation of Americans.

With the departure from this region of the worst elements employed by these men, it was then my duty to ascertain whether danger to American life still existed. As you know, in the latter part of March I informed Americans that I would sanction their return, believing that danger to life, locally, within certain specified areas, had passed, but my sanction was disapproved by the Legation. The subsequent occurrence of the Nanking and other incidents caused the Legation to issue me instructions to concentrate Americans still left in the district at a point suitable for evacuation by American naval vessels. In response to inquiries, those instructions have been repeated.

As the situation now stands, therefore, I must consider that my superior officers regard the conditions on the Yangtze as offering the possibility of trouble of such magnitude as to make the complete evacuation of Americans from all Nationalist-controlled territories advisable. In consonance with these instructions, therefore, I have asked Americans in this district so to reduce their numbers as to make prompt evacuation on an American destroyer possible, and to concentrate on the Island of Nantai. In justice to those whose duties required them to remain until the last, I also urged all non-essential persons to leave.

Such has been my official point of view. Regarding the point of view of those who accepted my advice, you doubtless know better than I, but I believe the majority belief was that it was the duty of Americans to take such action as would eliminate the necessity of intervention in the affairs of China by the American Government. Apropos of such an attitude, there is room for speculation as to different action our Government might have found itself able to take, following the Nanking affair, had not an American citizen—one who had been advised to leave but did not—been killed.

While the present position of this Consulate, on the question of further evacuation or the return of those who have left, is one where it must await further instructions, which will presumably be based on developments elsewhere in China, I should like, before leaving this question, to give you a brief glimpse into the present actual situation locally, even under the so-called "Moderate regime." I can do no better than send you, as enclosures to this letter, copies of an exchange of notes between this office and the Commissioner for Foreign Affairs. The facts, as shown in that correspondence and which will subsist, are that the authorities have not made and decline to make any restitution for past outrages; they have not only not returned but have continued to seize American private property; they have declined to give any guarantees of religious liberty or of protection for American missionary schools; they have declined to recognize existing treaty agreements between China and the United States. Thus, should Americans decide to return, under existing conditions, they must expect to be liable to forcible seizure of their properties; to a denial of the privilege of teaching the Christian religion; and to carry on without any charter or privilege other than the caprice of a constantly changing governmental personnel. Your Society must itself decide whether funds contributed for the propagation of the Christian religion can attain their object under such conditions. That is a matter outside my official province. I can only tell you what conditions actually are, in addition to telling you what my present instructions are.

THE PROTECTION OF AMERICAN INTERESTS

As previously stated, the American Government looks to the Chinese Government—and this includes any local *de facto* Government—for the primary protection of its citizens in China, and of their interests. I believe

THE SITUATION IN CHINA 67

I have made it sufficiently clear that, at least at present, the American Government is not disposed to attempt to protect its citizens in this district by force, and that it is at least extremely doubtful whether the *de facto* Government in this region is either willing or able to protect Americans and their interests. Not only is there not yet stability in the struggle between opposing forces within the Nationalist Government, but also there is unquestionably current throughout all parties a belief that certain forms of foreign enterprise in China conflict with fundamental tenets of the Nationalist faith. One of these forms is private educational enterprise. Whether or not your Society decides to place its properties and funds under the control of Chinese organizations is a purely private matter and outside my jurisdiction, but I wish to state as clearly as possible what I consider would be the actual legal status of such enterprises as are put under the control of persons or organizations not American. Presumably, the transfer of control would involve either the gift or the temporary and restricted use of certain real properties, such as school buildings. In either case, your Society would lose the right to American consular interposition on behalf of the organization, as such, and, even in the case of properties rented or loaned, it would be extremely difficult for the Consulate, once such arrangement were made, to interpose to protect your owner's interest. I believe that, so long as the property were not in actual danger of destruction or injury, you would have no right to request the interposition of the Consulate except for the ejection of the lessees for non-fulfillment of contract. For example, should the organization as such—as, let us say, Anglo-Chinese College under Chinese management and control—offend the law, it would be the Chinese Government that would hear the case, and Chinese law applied. A case of that sort has already occurred, in which the British Consul complained to the local authorities—on my denial of jurisdiction—against the behavior of certain of the students. In prosecuting such a case, the local authorities would have the right, I think, without consulting me, to enter any of the Anglo-Chinese properties, and take any action short of damaging or destroying the property in seeking out the offenders and punishing them. While such action was not taken, it is clear that conditions might well arise where one political faction might utilize such a complaint to work off a grudge against another faction, or where a group determined on closing out the school would utilize the opportunity for doing so.

In short, the situation would be simply that, whereas institutions which formerly were American could and did invoke consular aid in many of their problems, they could not do so after control has passed to Chinese. You could only invoke consular aid, as the owner of the property for the ejection of the lessees for breach of contract. It must be obvious that such ejection, even granting the sympathetic cooperation of the local authorities, would be extremely difficult to effect.

RELATIONS WITH *de facto* AUTHORITIES

I should like to add a word, in closing, on this subject. The treaties between China and the United States are valid and part of the law of each country. It is not within the legal competence of any American citizen to break those treaties. One of the provisions of the treaties—which, I might add, is part of usual international practice—is that an American citizen can communicate with the local authorities only through his Consul. Such a provision has its obvious virtue in limiting the relationship of States to certain accredited representatives, and also in obviating the creation of conflicting policies in such relationship. There is a reasonable limit, of course, within which this provision applies, but common sense should indicate what questions it would be advisable to refer or leave in the hands of accredited representatives. I shall raise only one. If and when your Society decides to transfer any of its agencies from the status of an American to a Chinese status, particularly when such transfer involves jurisdiction over physical properties, I would suggest that the Consulate be officially informed, and that the notification to the local Chinese authorities be left to the Consul. It takes a skilled acrobat to ride two horses; and in international relations the feat is impossible. Your agencies cannot have a dual status; they cannot be both American and Chinese. They must choose which they will be; and I suggest it is both just and in reasonable conformity with the treaties that the Consulate be the first to be informed of any change in status.

I fear this letter is over-long, but I felt you would like to have as careful a description as possible of the attitude of the Consulate toward some of the aspects of the present situation.

Very sincerely yours,

ERNEST B. PRICE,
American Consul.

Exhibit M.

A STATEMENT TO THE AMERICAN BOARD AND TO THE CONGREGATIONAL CHURCHES IN AMERICA

Most of the missionaries of the North China Mission, with the exception of those located in Peking and Tunghsien, are now in Tientsin or on their way to places outside the country, summoned on consular advice and that of our General Secretary. An informal meeting of the available members of the Mission then in Tientsin was held April 11-13. Thirty-two were present, the following statement was adopted, one voting in the negative and one refraining from voting.

I. THE BEARING OF THE INTERNATIONAL SITUATION ON OUR POLICY

a. Those of us who have already withdrawn from our stations have been influenced by some or all of the following considerations:

1. The Trend of Mission Thinking. For several years, the trend of opinion and feeling in our Mission, like that in the American Board, has been sympathetic toward the national aspirations of China and against foreign military pressure being used in China in this time of struggle and difficulty, although a few members of the Mission may even yet feel that the expression of our attitude should be left to our governmental authorities. As early as 1922, a group of twenty-four in our Mission began serious study of our relations to the international problems, and after repeated revisions of statements, which only a part of the group signed, a final statement was signed by all in March, 1924, and was sent to the American Minister in Peking. In part it read as follows: "We express our earnest desire that no form of military pressure, especially not foreign military force, be exerted to protect us or our property . . . . no punitive expedition be sent out and no indemnity be exacted. We take this stand believing that the way to establish righteousness and peace is through suffering wrong without retaliation and through bringing the spirit of good will to bear on all persons under all circumstances . . . . In signing this statement, we are all agreed in declaring against the use of armed foreign force and diplomatic threats or indemnities collected by our government."

Though this position was not supported by the Mission as a whole, after the May, 1925, incident in Shanghai, the sentiment in favor of a more general expression of our attitude grew rapidly, and during the autumn of that year, the statement given below was signed by a large majority of the Mission and in December was sent to the American Board in Boston. Additional signatures were obtained early in 1926, so that it was signed by 111 members of the North China Mission, all but six or seven then on the field who had been in China as long as a year:

"We, the undersigned, conceive it to be part of our task, while in China, to help to create and develop mutual understanding between the various races which come into contact with one another, to try to remove causes of international friction, and to stand for the highest type of international justice.

THE SITUATION IN CHINA

"Finding, in the treaties between our country and China, clauses which we believe hinder the realization of these aims, we desire to take a definite stand in regard to them. We do this in full loyalty to our own government, with a desire to see expressed in China the principles of honor and fair-play which we believe to be characteristic of the best nationals of our own lands.

"We therefore state it to be our purpose to use such influence as we have, both with our governments and our Mission Boards, toward securing as speedily as the necessary adjustments can be made, the modification of all treaties which infringe on the sovereignty or hinder the progress of China, and to urge that immediate steps be taken which will lead to restoring full tariff autonomy and the withdrawal of the privileges of extra-territoriality granted to foreign residents.

"Our sense of responsibility is deepened by the conviction that for Christian missions and missionaries longer to work under special rights and privileges, granted in the toleration clauses of the treaties, is not in accord with Christian principles, and we therefore wish to urge our governments to take decisive steps toward their early removal."

In February, 1926, conviction in the Mission was still stronger, and 106 members out of a total of 114 who are American citizens (the two Swiss nationals also signing) sent a cable to the American Board endorsing a cable which had just been sent by the Executive Committee of the National Christian Council, expressing the desire to place Chinese-American relations on a "cordial, reciprocal, equal basis" by immediately negotiating a new treaty, and to avoid as much as possible military measures during negotiations. Recent events have made temporary withdrawal from China the only logical outcome of this attitude and of our deepening convictions.

2. The attitude of the American Government toward Protection. While this feeling has been growing in the Mission, the State Department at Washington and diplomatic circles in China have alike insisted that the duty of the American Government to protect its citizens and their property and to secure indemnification in case of loss is absolute, at least to the extent of their ability, and in no wise affected by the geographical situation of the citizens or by their own desires not to be protected. To remain in China in the face of uncertainty as to developments means, therefore, to run the risk of involving the governments of China and the United States in diplomatic or military complications.

3. In most of the stations, upon receipt of advice from the consul, the missionaries consulted with the best-informed Chinese associates to ascertain their attitude toward their remaining or withdrawing. It was then uncertain what action our government might take with regard to the Nanking incident, but it was, in general, the judgment of the Chinese consulted that in case of disturbance or crisis, the presence of foreigners would prove more of an embarrassment than an aid, although there was question in some stations as to whether such disturbances were imminent in that locality. Most missionaries would have felt it their duty to remain in their stations, in spite of personal danger and consular orders, if they had believed that thereby they could render service in encouraging their associates and carrying on the work that would counter-balance risk of personal danger, involving international complications in the event that anything happened to them.

b. In view of the situation as described above and the cabled advice of the American Board, it was decided on April 11 that all whose furloughs were not already voted should withdraw to Korea and await developments, but this action will be referred for consideration to the Council which is meeting April 20.

1. In taking this action, all but three of our members present voted for this policy from a deep conviction that our best service to China and the cause of Christianity in China can be rendered only by withdrawal for a time from the country, thereby lessening to that extent the responsibility of our government for the protection of mis-

sionaries and the liability that our presence will create ill-will and provoke other unfortunate incidents with international complications. We feel that our continued presence endangers the ultimate attainment, through a remaking of the national life, of the peace and welfare of China, and delays the day when China shall have won her full place in the family of nations on a basis of self-respecting sovereignty. We express our willingness to return and share with our Chinese co-workers the joys and hardships of the period of reconstruction, but we at present strongly feel that the work of foreign missionaries in China will, in its largest implications, be futile until we are freed from the incubus of extra-territoriality and the toleration clauses in the treaties.

2. A second group in the Mission feels that, even though remaining in the work may lead to later diplomatic complications between China and America, there will be no possibility of American armed intervention in their behalf because of their distance from treaty ports, and the help and encouragement they can render to the Chinese Church in the present crisis seem to them to outbalance in importance the avoidance of possible causes of international complications.

3. For as long a period as may be desired by the Chinese churches, we feel it necessary to maintain the financial and business services now rendered by the business office, whether by the presence in Tientsin of one of the missionaries or by other suitable arrangements, but this whole question is being left to the Council.

II. THE BEARING OF OUR ACTION ON THE CHINESE CHURCH

In the minds of many of us, there is also a feeling that such a withdrawal will have more than a negative value. For five years, the anti-Christian movement has based its animosity on the supposed foreign and imperialistic elements in Christianity in China. For a longer period, the movement for an indigenous Church has felt itself hampered by what has seemed, in some Churches and Missions far more than in others, a reluctance to hand over a due share of responsibility to the Chinese Church and to local boards of managers of institutions. By the developments of the last few months, several conservative Missions have been forced in a few days or weeks to give into the inexperienced hands of their Chinese associates responsibilities which up to this time have been almost entirely borne by foreign missionaries. In the North China Congregational Union, the progressive evolution of fifteen years has given us in every station a group of experienced Chinese leaders, to whom we are now passing over the full responsibility for the work in church, school and hospital. Because this is being done in a spirit of confidence on our part, and with consecration and a deep sense of the responsibilities involved on the part of our Chinese associates, we look forward with faith and hope to the future development of these churches and institutions, in the confident expectation that those of us, whose further aid as advisers and helpers may still be desired by the Chinese Church, will be on a far more natural basis and in a position to render far more effectual aid than ever in the past.

III. THE BEARING OF OUR ACTION ON THE AMERICAN BOARD SUPPORT OF THE WORK

With confidence in our Chinese associates growing out of our years of fellowship in Christian labor with them, we believe that it is even more than in the past the duty and privilege of the American Board and the Congregational churches to continue sympathy, prayer, and financial and other assistance to the churches in China, regardless of whether there are American representatives associated in the administration or not. This will be of high value in demonstrating that our Christian thinking and love have transcended the barriers of race and nationality in our common devotion to Christ and His Church in all the world.